D0046190

keeping the Honey in the Honeymoon

keeping the Honey in the Honeymoon

Pat Avanzini

Tulsa, Oklahoma

For emphasis, the author has placed selected words from the scripture quotations in italics.

Keeping the Honey in the Honeymoon
ISBN 1-878605-44-5

PO Box 917001
Ft. Worth, TX 76117-9001

Published by
Abel Press
PO Box 702357
Tulsa, OK 74170-2357

It has always been my desire that everyone—each of my children, all of my church members, and now, you—would experience a marriage relationship as wonderful as the one John and I share.

How much I loved John from the very beginning! He was so compassionate, loving, and kind, in spite of the peer pressure that tried to make him seem rough and tough. I looked beyond that exterior and saw in him exactly what my heart wanted. We fell in love when I was just sixteen years old, and from that day I never kissed another man. The love we have shared over the years has always been special, and now I have seen that kind of love in another young couple.

I dedicate this book to my granddaughter, Cassie, and her good husband, Michael Cleveland. Michael has many of the same sweet ways that John has. He is so considerate and thinks Cassie is the greatest. After three years of marriage, I see their relationship continue to grow sweeter and sweeter. Their love has even brought us a precious little great-granddaughter, Caylee Rose.

But I see something even greater in their lives. They have a head start, because they are learning how to keep the honey in their honeymoon at a much younger age than John and I did.

Cassie and Michael, you are becoming a loving example of marriage for the next generation, and I am very proud of you.

Contents

PART II ✣ *How Do I Get There from Here?*

PART III — *Be Ready for Anything*

Foreword

Patricia has picked the right time in our history to write a book on keeping marriages together and having a little honey on the way. Today when the marriage vows seem to mean very little to people and many live together without that sacred vow that God ordained, she has put together out of her own delightful marriage and those in her ministry with whom she has counseled, a most down-to-earth and workable formula to keep the honey in the marriage and to keep the juices of life flowing. The book delighted me, and I received from it, even after 62 years of my own marriage to the same man. She reminded me of the honey I've tasted all these years. This is a frank and truthful book based on the Word of God. Anyone who deeply desires to have his or her marriage to be a true success should read this book. It should become a reference book to read again and again to keep your marriage stable, especially when there are problems. Your entire marriage can be a honeymoon all the way. I love the book, and so will you.

—Evelyn Roberts

Introduction

Wouldn't it be wonderful if ten years into every marriage, we expected that relationship to be as fulfilling and uplifting for both husband and wife as it was in the first days of courtship? If there were no games, or jockeying for power and position? If each partner lovingly and automatically thought of the other first, and both realized that such a marriage created a nurturing haven for their children?

I think that is exactly the way God envisioned marriage when he created men and women. Of course, that was when the garden was green, and Adam and Eve had not yet bitten into the forbidden fruit. That single incident is still reverberating in our lives, even after thousands of years.

But we bear much of the responsibility. We are allowing our most sacred relationships on earth, our marriages, to be stolen and attacked by a secular society that has plenty of motivation to see us fail. And we, both churched and unchurched couples, are failing at marriage in record numbers.

But that's not the worst news. Our messy relationships, our dysfunctional homes and our poor, traumatized children have become the fuel that powers an enormous segment of this society. Think of all the psychologists, counselors and doctors who profit from our misery. What about the divorce attorneys, advocates for the marriage partners, advocates for the children, and even advocates for the pets? Then there are private detectives and judges, and the people who run legal aid centers, women's havens and foster homes for children who are too war-torn to survive without shelter. There are government offices designed to implement childcare, job training, and even to teach people how to groom themselves, respond to an alarm clock, and dress to go to work. And let's not forget the people who make *special* high-interest loans to women who are suddenly alone—those who sell the new cars, new furniture, new dreams, and promise they can heal the wounds of broken spirits and broken hearts.

Failed marriages are big business. Don't expect society to step in and help us out of our mess. If we were to start getting along and loving each other as we once made a vow to do, large numbers of our professional people would be out of work.

So, how does the world handle the broken marriage problem? That's easy. They feed it. They caress the myths, and plump up the pillows of dysfunction. They glamorize divorce, extended families and the "second time around."

Maybe you've noticed how situation comedies tend to focus on these failures and to encourage, even celebrate, "Plan B." Comics know some of the best jokes take potshots at mothers-in-law, PMS, the nagging characteristics of women, and the *wandering eyes* of men. They don't bother to explain that women and men are simply different.

I think women will do almost anything to have a safe, well-stocked and clean environment for their children. But when couples are young and struggling, sometimes there can be many things that conspire to eat up the funds needed for such a home. So when women continue to push for that goal, it might be construed as nagging.

Men, on the other hand, are conquerors by nature. It is within them to provide food and shelter for their families. That often means long hours at work and a dedication to the job that a young wife might not understand. It is very easy, given the jokes and deliberate misrepresentations of the world, for a young couple to get off on the wrong foot.

Soon they are bickering constantly. He says she's nagging, and she says he's never home to hear it. They have begun the slow and deliberate process of letting the *honey* drip out of their *honeymoon.*

And exactly what constitutes the honeymoon? According to *Webster's, it refers to the first month after marriage. The vacation period spent by a newly married couple in travel and recreation. Or it refers to the mutual affection of newlyweds, regarded as waning like the moon.*

I think it's a mistake to view the honeymoon as a single period of time. There's a honeymoon after the marriage, of course. But there is also a honeymoon with a new baby, a new home, and with each new job, accomplishment or move that a couple experiences.

Each of these honeymoon periods needs to be nurtured, understood, and kept alive. If a new baby simply means sleepless nights, a loss of physical attention to either marriage partner, and bills that can no longer be met, the honeymoon period with that child will end quickly. But if a couple prepares before the child is born, if they have educated and reasonable expectations about the changes the child will bring to their marriage, they will not be blindsided.

As a pastor, I have had the privilege of conducting many weddings, and I can't think of a single couple that started out planning to fail. But I've also been in the position of counseling multitudes of couples whose marriages were in trouble. Most of them wanted, at least at first, to make their marriages survive. But many of those marriages failed in spite of their efforts and my own advice. Why? Unfortunately, I believe it is because long before they ended up in my office, they had begun to let the *honey* drip out of their honeymoon.

In the beginning, I believe the damage is barely noticeable. Maybe one of them begins to leave the house without kissing the other goodbye. Maybe he doesn't want to wake her, or she is running late. But then the hugs become less frequent. The couple begins to argue over silly things. Then the arguments grow more intense and both of them harbor seeds of bitterness. They say things that cause deep wounds, and more and more of the precious honey drips out through these new lesions.

Happy couples do not just wake up one morning wanting a divorce. It comes from a little conflict here and a little conflict there. Line upon line, each incident steals more honey from the reservoir. And if no one steps in to stop the leaks, that marriage faces the inevitable torment of heartbreak and disappointment. It happens exactly as the Scriptures said it would. The little things end up spoiling the relationship. "*...the* *little foxes, that spoil the vines: for our vines have tender grapes."* Song of Solomon 2:15, KJV

Making honey and preserving honey are not easy tasks. Have you ever watched bees work on a summer afternoon? They go from flower to flower, gathering nectar, carrying it back to the hive, and then returning for another load. Why are they so dedicated? Because when winter winds blow and temperatures drop to freezing, the honey they have made will sustain the hive, keeping them all alive to enjoy another summer.

We need to realize marriage is hard work. Just like those bees, we have to sustain the honey in our homes, our families and our marriage relationships. When we occasionally face challenges and hard times, we can't quit. We must keep a reservoir of honey, something to fall back on, to help us remember *when* we fell in love, *why* we fell in love, and the *value* of keeping the covenants we have made.

God wants our marriages to grow sweeter with every year. If you will read this book with a willing heart and practice the things you learn, it has the power to make a new marriage blossom into strength, to help resurrect a faltering marriage, and to see you all the way to the silver and golden anniversaries where you will discover that *God has saved the sweetest honey for last.*

My husband, John, has encouraged me to write this book for many years. Why? Because marriages have always been an important part of our ministry. On a personal level, I have pastored people or been a pastor's wife for more than thirty-five years. I have counseled couples and individuals, studied dozens of marriage textbooks and attended countless seminars and classes. But my greatest credential for writing about marriage is my own relationship. I have been married to John for forty-five years. He is the force behind this book; he makes me believe I can accomplish anything. He is my best friend, my confidant, and the person who knows me better than anyone else on earth.

I want to thank him—here, publicly—for encouraging me in everything I attempt to do. John never gives up on me. Better than that, he never lets me give up on myself. He is the only man who has ever been in my life. I love him more than I can express. He's every fantasy, every dream I had as a young girl, only better. His arms comfort me; his smile renews me. He has become so deep a part of me that I cannot imagine life without him. It seems inadequate to say that I love him. Because there is so much more to our relationship, so much more to who we are as a couple, as parents, as pastors.

My wish for you as you read this book is that you might experience the same kind of marriage that John and I have found, a sharing and caring that is greater than any problem or challenge you could face in life.

I pray that by the time you finish this book, you will understand God's perfect will for your marriage, and you will be built up and prepared to withstand the attacks of the enemy—and the world—that will try to come against you and your spouse.

Part I

The Way it is Meant to be

Chapter 1

Marriage, The Way It Is Meant To Be

The Beginning

Marriage is designed to be wonderful. Two people with shared goals, deep love, and a joy in being together. Friends. It's really that simple. So when did we make it complicated? When did we start fussing over bills, kids, in-laws, chores, and sex? When did we turn this marvelous relationship into a war, and start letting judges and attorneys referee the battles?

Nearly all couples start out starry-eyed and in love. They may not be thinking about goals or friendship. They simply want to spend all their time together. Even when older and more experienced people try to warn them about pitfalls and prepare them for possible trouble, they usually think they can beat the odds. They believe their love is so true, so special, that they will never argue, let alone seek a divorce.

Maybe that's part of the problem. Young love is so sweet and so beautiful that most people decide to just let the newlyweds find out for themselves what it's like to share a bathroom, get up early in the morning for work, field phone calls about overdue bills, and later, deal with the reality of birthing and raising children. I wonder if that's wise. Many young adults enter marriage with completely unrealistic expectations.

They have preconceived ideas of how things will be handled in the home—based on behavior they saw and learned as they grew up. Many do not have a clear idea of what a husband's role or a wife's role should be. Many years ago, John and I invited a man in his early twenties to stay in our home for three weeks. We had five children, four of them teenagers, and we were living in a four-bedroom house with two bathrooms. We had just taken a new pastorate and finances were very tight. The situation was stressful to say the least.

In a home that size with a family of seven, what we lived is what he saw. I always imagined it was as difficult for him as it was for us, but apparently it wasn't. Twenty years later we heard from him. By that time he was a mature pastor. He told us that those three weeks, that brief time in our overcrowded home, were the only example he ever had of a husband's and a father's role. It made me realize we never know how or to what degree we are impacting others as we go through life.

With all the misinformation and the confusion that newlyweds bring to their unions, we should not be surprised that they sometimes stumble. When life, with its inherent emotions, problems, conflicts and struggles, arrives the week after the honeymoon ends, a lot of young people think they have made a terrible mistake. It has to be a mistake, right? Love is supposed to last forever. Knights ride in wearing their shining armor, and they whisk their ladies off into the sunset. No one ever prepared them for bills, high rents, escalating grocery costs, car repairs, minimum wage, and the many other details that suddenly become daily challenges.

Where did happily-ever-after go? Where did Prince Charming go? Where's that beautiful little bride who always agreed with every word that came out of her young lover's mouth?

For many couples, these questions, these conflicts, arise within a month of the wedding, and can linger forty or fifty years or longer. And once the problems arise, the dissatisfaction, the anger and the blame-game begin. If a wife doesn't cook, clean, or dress like people on television, she must be doing something wrong. If a husband doesn't help out with the chores, earn a high wage, and bring flowers and candy to his wife at the end of the day, he isn't doing his part.

Remember those early days of courting when he asked, "Where shall we go, Honey?" And she replied, "Oh, Sweetie, that's up to you. Anything you want to do is all right with me." That can wear thin after a while. If one of them always gives over to the other, always preferring to do what the other spouse wants, a deep resentment can build. That is a natural reaction that can cause a feeling of poor self-image, a sense of being inferior.

All of these problems are the fruit of unrealistic expectations. When young men and women form their ideas of marriage from romance novels, television sit-coms, movies, books and even pornography, no real-life man or woman will ever live up to the fantasy. It is time that we begin to teach our young people about biblical marriage, what God designed the marriage relationship to be, and what He expects from each of them.

And it's not just young people that need this information. Because people of all ages have been raised with false hopes, ideas, and expectations, the world (church families included) is filled with bad marriages, failed marriages, re-marriages, second families, third families, extended families, broken families, and families that have just about lost hope.

It wasn't supposed to be that way. God designed something very different. He never said it would be easy. But He did design it to be fun, exhilarating, and deeply rewarding.

I have found the joy; I have experienced the rewards; I have learned a lot about the things it takes to have a happy marriage. But even that wasn't enough to qualify me to speak on this subject. I needed to wait another twenty years, so I could discover what it was like to have grown children, to see the struggles and the victories as they were experienced by another generation.

This book isn't meant to have the soft, easy flow of fiction. It's not a romance novel. It's better than that. It is truth. It will speak to you honestly, sharing some of the secrets John and I have learned, a bit of wisdom that was hard won, and a lot of common sense that can help couples build marriages that will be rich and fulfilling.

Prince Charming, Godly Homes, and Happily Ever After

As early as I can remember, I had dreams and expectations about marriage. When I was young, I remember wondering, "Where will I meet the man of my dreams? What will he look like? Where will we live? How many children will we have?" I was like most young Christian girls. All my ideas of marriage were idealistic and romantic—Prince Charming, a godly home with the husband taking the role of spiritual leadership, and happy endings.

God's ways, His thoughts and timing are very different from ours. In the midst of all my dreams about marriage, I also had a desire to go to Baylor University. So when I met John Avanzini, marriage was nowhere near the front burner of my life. He wasn't the kind of boy I dated. He drank; he smoked; and he was a little on the rowdy side. The first night we met, he and his friends decided to buzz past my house after I'd gone home. They also decided it would be funny to throw all their beer cans on my parent's front lawn. Imagine the impression that made.

I was the first child in my family, and my parents were very strict. I wanted to go out with John, and I knew I needed my parent's permission to do that. But no matter how hard I tried, I could not get that name Avanzini to flow off my tongue. I had trouble pronouncing it, so I introduced him to my family as John Brown. Once they got to know him, they loved him. John has a wonderful sense of humor, and he is one of the kindest men I have ever known.

I remember when we would come home from dates, we weren't allowed to spend much time sitting out in the car. My parents would flip the porch light and we would get out of the car, go stand on the porch and start talking. My dad would begin to sing, "Goodnight, Sweetheart, well it's time to go." I can laugh about that now. My parents were simply showing their love and their desire to keep me from making a mistake. I was just as strict with my own children later.

Because I was a Christian, I was concerned that John wasn't saved. I had been taught in church youth class that this was a very important issue. I knew he would have to change if we were to continue in our relationship. These days, I am amazed how many parents and young adults do not realize the importance of that advice. The Bible tells us in 2 Corinthians 6:14, *"Do not be unequally yoked together with unbelievers. For what fellowship has righteousness with lawlessness? And what communion has light with darkness?"* NKJV

Because it was so important to me that John find salvation, he finally pretended to get saved. And just as honeymoons wear off, so did his salvation. My advice to young people: Don't just believe someone if he tells you he has gotten saved. Be a fruit inspector. The Word says, *"By their fruit you will recognize them. Do people pick grapes from thornbushes, or figs from thistles? Likewise every good tree bears good fruit, but a bad tree bears bad fruit"* Matthew 7: 16-17, NIV.

I know it was God's will for John and I to fall in love with each other. And I rejoice that He did not forget my prayers for a Christian husband and father for my children, although He certainly could have thought *I* forgot.

Once John and I got married, we relocated from our small town to Houston, Texas. Being young and madly in love, finding a church was not a top priority in our lives. We found a Methodist church and started attending, but going to church and developing into the image of Christ are two different things. Even though John got involved with their building program, he was still as lost as a goose in a snowstorm.

Let me praise God, as I have for many, many years. I thank Him for His love and the care He has shown over my life, for the salvation of my good husband, and for the joy of being called into the Lord's work, even though that's not how we started.

As the years passed, my grandmother died. She was a very godly woman. Her death stirred my spirit, and I realized how much I missed the closeness I once had with the Lord. I started attending church again, taking our first child with me and leaving the baby home with John. During that year, John's grandmother died also. As he contemplated her death, new feelings about God began to stir in him, and God chose that perfect moment to send a construction worker named

Lester Miller to minister to him. That man was instrumental in John's decision to finally give his life to the Lord.

At last a few pieces of the puzzle came together. We could begin to see what was required for a happy (godly) marriage. We started our lives together in the Lord with two children and a third on the way. We finally had the key that would unlock the doors to a fulfilled marriage, a godly family life, and a sense of peace we had not known.

Not that it became easy. There were many times when I wanted to throw in the towel and call it quits, but I'm so glad I didn't. A long marriage is something to treasure, and it's well worth the time and effort required. I didn't achieve that in my life without learning a lot, giving a lot, and, of course, receiving a lot in return. We have experienced trials, and we have both had to learn to give and to forgive—not only each other, but also ourselves.

We have learned so much during the years we have been together. So I encourage you, please don't give up. Keep trying. Seek God's wisdom and knowledge, His plan. Everyone can and will make mistakes. We all have occasional flashes of temper. We say things we shouldn't, things we don't really mean. When that happens, we need to forgive ourselves and begin again.

I have learned to confront issues rather than simply overlooking them. Yes, it leads to friction, but that can be a good thing. It causes rough edges to be rubbed off so we can be "fitly joined together" (Ephesians 4:16). In the same way that we sometimes have to use Liquid Plumber to clear our plumbing, a good confrontation can keep the communication lines open.

Now after forty-five years of marriage, after all the disagreement, frustration and tears, I am truly thankful we pressed on and didn't give up on each other. I continually remind myself that two can accomplish more than one, and God always saves the best wine for last. My desire for all my children, the people in my church, and for you is that you will be able to learn from my experiences and the experiences of others that I will share in these pages.

Don't Reinvent the Wheel

If you know people who have already discovered secrets and shortcuts to the joy found in a happy marriage, I advise you to listen to them. You don't have to figure out everything on your own. If I had to describe the most important key to a good marriage, other than putting God first in life and following His will, I would say that agreement is the one thing that will help any marriage. As couples, we need to be in agreement with each other about how and when we will spend our money, how we will raise our children, our marriage goals and priorities, and all the other details that will impact our lives. Once we have discussed these things, once we reach agreement about how important each issue will be, we will have more peace in our lives. It really works. I have sweet feelings for my precious Johnny, even as I write. These wonderful feelings come because we have kept our communication lines open.

Too often we decide on things without rhyme or reason, dealing with them as they come up instead of planning ahead: how many children we want, what kind of home we plan to work toward, what kinds of friends we will have, and whether or not Christianity will be a priority in our lives. Is it any surprise that we begin to argue once we discover we have completely opposite opinions on many of these issues?

Agreement will save years of pain. Please take it from someone who has learned the hard way. In order to get into agreement, you must have conversation. Conversation is communication—plain talking—sharing. It defeats the element of surprise. If a young wife wants four children and her husband thinks one is all he can handle or afford, they need to know this information. If the young husband enjoys weekend barbeques, volleyball and tennis, and his wife prefers quiet candlelight dinners for two and an occasional evening at the ballet, they need to find a common ground. If one of them sees a 1500 square-foot rambler as the ultimate dream home, but the other has visions of a sprawling two-story with a commanding view of the sea, they need to talk.

Good marriages do not just happen. They are a lot of work. I know we live in a world with microwaves, instant this and instant that, but a good marriage takes time and effort. It happens only when both husband and wife are willing to compromise and not insist on having their own way. God gave us the minds, hearts and intelligence to achieve the level of communication that brings true happiness.

It is God's will that you enjoy a happy marriage. Marriage does not have to become boring and unexciting like the world advertises and says in its books, television shows, and movies. It does not have to be a war zone or a battleground where the children flex their muscles and control every evening at the dinner table. It does not have to be a "He said/She said" war of the sexes, nor does there ever have to be another argument about money, the concern of an aging physique, the never-ending diets, or the next situation with the children. Bitterness can be a thing of the past when God's plan for a marriage becomes the standard in a home. Let me say one more time: keep on trying. It just gets sweeter and sweeter.

God wasn't the least bit shy about letting people know what He expected from them in marriage. Once a man and a woman seek God's will, follow His instructions about courtship, and become convinced He desires them to marry, once they get into agreement about the part God will play in their marriage, His peace, joy, and love can create a fruitful environment where precious little ones will thrive.

The First Marriage

As soon as God created man, He knew something was missing. The man would be lonely. The man, with his masculine characteristics, would need a counterpart, someone to soften his hunter's heart, someone to help him appreciate the beauty of the earth and show him the wisdom of weeping at the magnificence of a sunset or a newborn child.

So God created woman. He called her man's "helpmeet." And with that creation, He set into motion the most challenging, rewarding, wondrous and uplifting relationship that would ever exist on earth: marriage.

I have a hunch it was challenging back then, too. For example, let's say Adam loved bananas. Perhaps he grabbed Eve's hand and rushed to share the wonder of bananas with her. But what if she didn't like them? What if she preferred plums? Or apples? First opportunity for hurt feelings! Adam might have felt insecure because this woman God gave him didn't appreciate the miracle of bananas. Even in the Garden of Eden it could have happened. The first argument.

Perhaps that first disagreement took longer than that but remember, Adam and Eve were human. After they ate the forbidden fruit, what if Eve didn't care for the fig leaf Adam brought her to wear? What if she thought it made her look fat? She might have preferred palm fronds with their horizontal lines and the majestic size that couldn't help but dwarf her. You can bet they found things to fuss about. Like why they were suddenly tossed out of the garden. "You ate it first," Adam must have sputtered. "Yes, but you are my covering," Eve could have answered. "Why didn't you stop me?"

Maybe if they had paused right then, right there in the beginning, maybe if they had taken the time to seek God's will for their relationship, they could have saved all of us from following them right down that willful and rebellious trail they blazed.

But they didn't. Shame came upon them; they covered their nakedness, and they were evicted from the Garden. From that very moment, we have been forced to deal with shame, deception and all the other things that old serpent, Satan, introduced.

By the way, what did Satan get out of that incident? Exactly what he wanted. He wanted their marriage. He wanted their attention. He wanted them to think God was somehow cheating them because they couldn't eat ALL the fruit in the Garden. He was telling a lie, but he didn't care. He introduced the first idea that God does not have our best interests at heart. He was the first to insinuate that God is a God of *can't* instead of *can*. And you know, his goals haven't changed. He hasn't let up on marriages a bit since that day.

He still assaults us in our homes, telling wives that husbands don't communicate, that they just don't care, and telling husbands that wives are constant nags, impossible to please, and that all that weeping and emotion just gets in the way of a good marriage. He fills our days with negative stories in the newspapers, cynical shows on television, insulting and sexist jokes from comics, insensitive movies, and profane exploitations of the marriage relationship in every form of media.

Adam and Eve messed things up rather quickly. Even so, God's Word still speaks to us about His initial desire for marriage. In Hebrews 13:4, the Word says, *"Let marriage be held in honor (esteemed worthy, precious, of great price, and especially dear) in all things. And thus let the marriage bed be undefiled (kept undishonored); for God will judge and punish the unchaste [all guilty of sexual vice] and adulterous"* (Amplified Bible).

God says marriage is a holy union between two people. He designed it to be a source of joy, love and balance. It should be esteemed and considered precious. Godly marriages are divine relationships. The marriage vows involve serious commitments, commitments that are meant to last a lifetime.

Unfortunately, many couples enter marriage with the attitude, "Well, if it doesn't work out, we'll just get a divorce." Or, "Let's try it for a while and see if it works." What do you imagine God thinks of pre-nuptial agreements? How can marriages last when newlyweds are planning for the way out before they find their way in?

I think it's time we begin to teach young people that marriage is a lifetime commitment with unconditional love. Jesus talked about that in the Book of Matthew. The Pharisees had approached Him with the express purpose of tripping Him up and making Him say something that conflicted with Old Testament Law. *"Now it came to pass, when Jesus had finished these sayings, that He departed from Galilee and came to the region of Judea beyond the Jordan. And great multitudes followed Him, and He healed them there. The Pharisees also came to Him, testing Him, and saying to Him, "Is it lawful for a man to divorce his wife for just any reason?" And He answered and said to them, "Have you not read that He who made them at the beginning 'made them male and female,' and said, 'For this reason a man shall leave his father and mother and be joined to his wife, and the two shall become one flesh'? So then, they are no longer two but one flesh. Therefore what God has joined together, let not man separate"* Matthew 19: 1-6, NKJV.

That is the heart of the Father. God is the originator of marriage, and He created it to be a permanent union. In the mind of God, divorce should not even be in a Christian's vocabulary.

Now I want to pause right here and say something. God's desire is for us to have holy unions. Jesus was talking about marriage as the Father designed it to be. Sometimes people, men and women alike, abuse their mates. Whether that abuse is physical or emotional, God did not plan for any of His children to live a life of abuse. Let this sink in and don't forget it. There are legitimate reasons that some marriages cannot be saved. For those who have prayerfully submitted their situations to the Lord, just know that God does not want you to suffer humiliation, injury or any other form of abuse.

I want to mention one other thing. We are talking about God's blessings on the marriage relationship. I am not saying that God does not bless single people. Indeed, He does. But that relationship needs to be covered in another book. This book is for married people, written to discuss the many revelations and insights into marriage that God has shown me and others over the years.

God's Way Makes the Way

Many people disagree with the fact that marriage is God's plan. Instead, they want to make their own rules and live as they please. The results in our society have been devastating. Because of rejecting God's plan, countless lives have been literally destroyed.

When I turn on the television, I am continually bombarded by the world's casual attitude toward sex outside the marriage relationship. It is no wonder that most nations are experiencing escalating divorce rates. With promiscuity running wild, it is also not surprising that we are plagued with AIDS and other sexually transmitted diseases. This was never God's plan for us.

We should never yield to the thinking of those who say, "Everyone else is doing it." Or, "If you love someone, premarital (or extramarital) sex is okay." The Lord can give you the strength, courage, and determination to keep yourself pure no matter what the temptation or circumstance. The Bible even says there is no temptation too powerful for you to resist. *"No temptation has overtaken you except such as is common to man; but God is faithful, who will not allow you to be tempted beyond what you are able, but with the temptation will also make the way of escape, that you may be able to bear it"* 1 Corinthians 10:13, NKJV.

God designed sex to be an enjoyable part of the marriage relationship. There is nothing nasty or ungodly about it. God created our bodies to enjoy sexual activity. If He did not intend for sex to be enjoyed, He would never have made it so pleasurable. The Bible even tells husbands and wives not to deprive each other of sexual satisfaction. *"Let the husband render to his wife the affection due her, and likewise also the wife to her husband. The wife does not have authority over her own body, but the husband does. And likewise the husband does not have authority over his own body, but the wife does. Do not deprive one another except with consent for a time, that you may give yourselves to fasting and prayer; and come together again so that Satan does not tempt you because of your lack of self-control* 1 Corinthians 7: 3-5, NKJV.

That seems pretty clear to me.

Why would the Bible tell people not to deprive their spouses of sexual pleasure? By using the word *deprive,* God made it clear that sex was something married people have a right to enjoy. In counseling, I have encountered many people who withheld sex from their spouses just because they didn't enjoy it. Others, often women, withheld sex because they felt it was the only thing their husbands took an interest in. Whatever the reason, it is ungodly and unscriptural for a married person to withhold sexual fulfillment from his or her spouse.

When it comes to sex outside marriage, God didn't leave any room for uncertainty or gray areas. We already read what He had to say, but let's look at it again. *"Let marriage be held in honor (esteemed worthy, precious, of great price, and especially dear) in all things. And thus let the marriage bed be undefiled (kept undishonored); for God will judge and punish the unchaste [all guilty of sexual vice] and adulterous"* Hebrews 13:4, Amplified Bible.

What is the message here? God is telling us that sexual relationships outside of marriage are against His will. They are not only unscriptural, they will cause destruction in the lives of those who pursue them. Additionally, the Word says, *"Do you not know that the unrighteous will not inherit the kingdom of God? Do not be deceived. Neither fornicators, nor idolaters, nor adulterers, nor homosexuals, nor sodomites, nor thieves, nor covetous, nor drunkards, nor revilers, nor extortioners will inherit the kingdom of God"* 1 Corinthians 6: 9-10, NKJV.

Unfortunately for those who are always looking for loopholes, they won't find any here. God didn't leave room for doubt. He doesn't want us involved in infidelity, and He does not approve of living with people before we get married. There are reasons. God knows those things lead to heartbreak, loss of respect, low self-esteem, unwanted children, and many other things that keep us from enjoying the happiness He planned for us. God is not cruel. He has made these rules (as well as all the Ten Commandments) for the same reasons we don't allow our children to run in the street, play with matches or wander anywhere they like after dark.

Disobedience to God's ordinances can literally destroy people. The damage caused by an unfaithful partner can inflict permanent damage on everyone involved. And with the advent of AIDS, an unfaithful spouse can kill a husband or wife, or condemn an unborn child to death by this dreadful disease. Isn't it a shame how we have messed up God's wonderful plans for us?

Sin cloaks itself in temptation. Look at the lights in Las Vegas.

Look at the commercials for tobacco, alcohol and other vices. Madison Avenue is clever. Ads showing healthy, happy people dancing and enjoying life are a good way to sell products. What kind of commercial would it be if tobacco ads showed a person ravaged by lung cancer and dying alone in a darkened room? Or an alcoholic passed out in an alley—family, reputation and hope all gone?

Sin seems good for a season. The devil traps his victims by making things look wonderful and inviting, but he always fails to show the end result. Never forget that the Bible warns us of this very thing. "*For the wages of sin is death...*" Romans 6:23a, NKJV.

When a man and a woman exchange their wedding vows and say, "I do," they enter a covenant with more than each other. They make that covenant before God. They are also saying "I do" to Him. And those vows are a serious matter to the Lord.

The devil likes to hide sin under other names. Instead of adultery, the sin is now called an "affair." But whatever it's called, God knows our sins will destroy us from the inside out. And He'll never just look the other way. According to Proverbs 6: 32, "*Whoever commits adultery with a woman lacks understanding; He who does so destroys his own soul*" NKJV.

Sin may be fun for a while, but those who do not sincerely and fully repent pay a tremendous price. Moses knew that. The Word says, "*By faith Moses, when he was come to years, refused to be called the son of Pharaoh's daughter; Choosing rather to suffer affliction with the people of God, than to enjoy the pleasures of sin for a season*" Hebrews 11:24,25, KJV. How long is a season? Well, there are four seasons in a year, so a single season must last only about three months. Would we give up our eternal inheritance for three months of pleasure?

Marriage was instituted to be a source of joy and happiness for a man and a woman. I have noticed with John and myself, when one of us is having a bad day, the other can give encouragement. God never meant for us to be a burden to one another. He meant just the opposite, that we would be a blessing.

God wants our marriages to be full of love, happiness, and joy. If such a goal were impossible, He would not have spoken of that type of relationship. It just takes commitment, agreement, a knitting and bonding together, and a determination to get to know and trust one another. It is a process that takes time, but God meets us where we are and takes us on this wonderful journey through life.

It's a Matter of Choice

A successful marriage does require an act of your will. While we know God has the power to do all things, it is clear that we are not robots. He lets us make our own choices. Nowhere is this more true than in marriage. We can lavish our love, kindness and gentleness all over each other, or we can be real grumps and neglect one another's needs and desires. It is our choice.

I have discovered that daily decisions determine the degree of happiness a marriage produces. Those who invest in love and kindness eventually reap love and kindness. Those who choose to invest in strife and anger also reap what they sow.

Marriage is a covenant. A covenant is an agreement between two parties. We promise to love and honor each other, keep ourselves faithful from other sexual partners, and stand by each other in sickness and in health. When one partner (or both) begins to take these vows for granted and make compromises, that marriage is headed for trouble. But if we would simply remember the vows we made, make it a point to re-read them or perhaps even repeat them to each other periodically, a lot of marriage problems could be averted.

When your mate makes a mistake, forgets a birthday, breaks a promise, fails to be sensitive, there are two clear choices. Judgment is easy. Blame and shame take no effort. The hard choice—the other choice—is love. And choosing love doesn't come automatically until it has been practiced many times.

"Love is patient and kind. Love is not jealous or boastful or proud or rude. Love does not demand its own way. Love is not irritable, and it keeps

no record of when it has been wronged. It is never glad about injustice but rejoices whenever the truth wins out. Love never gives up, never loses faith, is always hopeful, and endures through every circumstance" 1 Corinthians 13: 4-7, TLB.

That is the kind of love God wants us to practice in our marriages. And if both partners walk in that kind of love, there will be very little chance their marriage will end in divorce. Does this sound like an impossible dream or a goal that can never be reached? Get that stinking thinking out of your mind. Nothing is impossible with God!

Through the power of the Holy Ghost, you can allow God to transform your mind and control your actions. Line upon line, precept upon precept, here a little, there a little, you can learn to walk in love and hardly notice when others do something wrong. Stop reading for a moment. With your eyes closed, try to imagine how fulfilling God meant marriage to be.

This kind of marriage takes a willing heart and a commitment to live righteously before God and the person you have married. It won't be easy, but the benefits will outweigh all the effort and struggles as a godly character begins to replace old ways of thinking.

There is no guarantee that both partners will realize the importance of change at the same time. One of them may have to take the initiative. Perhaps it will be a husband who gets under the teaching of a great and inspirational Christian leader. It might be a wife who hears a wise and loving speaker at a women's retreat or conference.

Even if one spouse chooses not to walk in love, there is hope. God will richly honor the efforts of a person who is trying to steer their marriage back to a godly standard. When one partner decides to do what is right, regardless of the choices made by the other, God is able to work in that marriage and in that family.

When people choose to let God rule their lives, they have better marriages. The devil will always be standing by, trying to cause strife and division. He knows he has lost, and he knows where he is going. He wants us to be losers, too, so he tries to tempt us to live according to the flesh. And since those days in the Garden, his special targets have been husbands and wives. Especially in Christian homes! But God has promised us victory. Those of us who will let the power and the love of God flow through our lives and our marriages will reap tremendous rewards. Satan's plans for destruction will fail, and God's plan for our marriages will prevail. Get this important little word: LET. We must *let* it happen.

Several years ago, John and I were traveling, and I found two poems that really blessed me. Since then, both poems have hung framed in our home, close to a picture of us. I always knew our golden years would come. I always understood that the choices I make every day affect the level of honey that John and I enjoy, even after forty-five years of marriage.

Following is one of those poems. I hope it blesses you as it has John and me.

Marriage Takes Three

I once thought marriage took
Just two to make a go,
But now I am convinced
It takes the Lord also.

And not one marriage fails
Where Christ is asked to enter
As lovers come together
With Jesus at the center.

In homes where Christ is first,
It's obvious to see
Those unions really work,
For marriage still takes three.

PERRY TANKSLEY

Chapter 2

Marriage is not for Sissies

One of the things I frequently hear from my mother-in-law is that growing old is not for sissies. I will say the same thing about marriage. Those people who choose to have a good, godly marriage and home have set themselves up in direct opposition to the enemy. Because of that, you can count on him to send one attack after another. It takes a lot of courage to stand against Satan on a daily basis and trust God for protection.

Satan wants to destroy marriages! It's that simple. *"Be sober, be vigilant; because your adversary the devil walks about like a roaring lion, seeking whom he may devour"* 1 Peter 5:8, NKJV.

What destroys most marriages? Is it financial problems, uncaring spouses, sexual problems, incompatibility, a home where the children rule, empty nests, obsessive diets, infidelity, or neglect? Certainly those are some of the issues that get the blame during marital disputes and even divorces. But all of these things are actually *symptoms* of a greater problem. When we work hard to correct such situations, we are often surprised to find we experience only temporary relief. Why? Because we have corrected the *symptom* instead of the problem.

Imagine you have a sinus infection caused by bacteria and you have the following symptoms: sneezing, a runny nose, and a sore throat. If you want temporary relief, you can go to a pharmacy and purchase a medication that will mask the symptoms. Your nose will stop running, but the bacteria are still in your system. Unless you take a medication that kills the source of the problem, you will have to deal with it until the infection runs its natural course, or God intervenes with a miracle and kills the bacteria.

It's the same with marriage problems. When we treat the symptoms (sexual problems, financial problems, incompatibility) without getting to the core issues, we are going to be disappointed.

The Devil and the Flesh

What are the real issues? The devil and the flesh. These two things produce most of the destructive and irritating symptoms that plague our marriages.

Uncontrolled flesh (natural desires, lust, lack of self-control, selfishness, greed, etc.) causes major problems in every form of relationship. In counseling sessions, I hear about the symptoms of uncontrolled flesh all the time. It has caused employers to abuse faithful employees. It has caused employees to steal from their companies, to give less than a hundred-percent effort, and to murmur about their employers. The flesh has destroyed friendships, ruined lives, and filled the courts to overflowing with painful and damaging stories.

Despite all these terrible things, nothing compares to the devastating damage that uncontrolled flesh can cause in marriages. It has caused husbands and wives to literally destroy each other with words. It has spawned unhappy homes, spousal abuse and divorce. Uncontrolled flesh is a bacteria the devil uses to infect our marriages, leaving trails of sickness (marital problems) and death (divorce).

Everyone who has spent time in the Word has been exposed to God's teachings on the characteristics of the Holy Spirit. They are often called the fruit of the Spirit. *"But the fruit of the Spirit is love, joy, peace, patience, kindness, goodness, faithfulness, gentleness and self-control. Against such things there is no law"* Galatians 5: 22-23. These are characteristics that we encourage every born-again child of God to produce.

But if there is fruit of the Spirit, wouldn't it stand to reason there is also fruit of the flesh? It is a Biblical principle. *"The acts of the sinful nature are obvious: sexual immorality, impurity and debauchery; idolatry and witchcraft; hatred, discord, jealousy, fits of rage, selfish ambition, dissensions, factions and envy; drunkenness, orgies, and the like. I warn you, as I did before, that those who live like this will not inherit the kingdom of God"* Galatians 5: 19-21.

These works of the flesh have the potential to cause major problems in our marriages. No one would argue with the fact that immorality causes marriage problems. But what about strife? Or jealousy and anger? They can be just as destructive to a marriage.

The Effects of Stubbornness

Please notice a couple things about the above verses. First of all, they say nothing about Satan. You might expect that such a list of evil things would include at least one reference to the devil, but it doesn't. Even though we know Satan has a goal of destroying marriages, we are making his job way too easy. Uncontrolled flesh is already chewing away at the very heart of many marriages.

Another thing, the fruit of the flesh listed in Galatians is not a complete list. Scripture adds, *"...and such like"* to the end of the inventory. That means our flesh can manifest additional characteristics, like stubbornness. Stubborn people are frequently persistent and unreasonable. They insist on having their own way, in spite of the tribulation it brings to their lives and the lives of others.

Think of the expression, "Stubborn as a mule." In the old days, farmers would use mules to plow their fields. If the mule decided not to plow anymore, he would simply stop—right in his tracks. The farmer could scream. He could even take out a whip and beat the mule, but that animal would not move an inch. The sad thing is that some people are just like that old mule. They refuse to change, even when they are being beaten by the devil.

I have talked to some people who are so stubborn that I believe the Lord Jesus Christ could appear in front of them and instruct them to change, and they would refuse. That sounds terrible, but it is true.

The Bible warns against that level of stubbornness. *"The man [or woman] who is often reproved but refuses to accept criticism will suddenly be broken and never have another chance"* Proverbs 29:1, TLB.

Again, God is clear in His speaking. He wants us to get the lessons He presents. The stubborn person is headed for danger. Some will never have the chance to make things right. I have witnessed that in marriage counseling. Some people have become so weary that even when their spouses promise to change, they simply cannot give them another chance.

Stubbornness is also contagious. If one spouse develops a stubborn spirit, it becomes easy for stubbornness to manifest itself in the other spouse. Once both partners have hardened their hearts, Satan has accomplished his goal, and strife rules in that home.

What should someone do about a stubborn spouse? Pray. Walk in love. Resist the selfishness that would grow out of a vengeful heart. By obeying God's Word and following His teachings, we allow Him the freedom to change the stubborn spouse.

The Effects of Selfishness

What about selfishness? If many marriages are lost to stubborn spirits and an unwillingness to give, many more fall under the grinding and relentless wheels of selfishness. In fact, I believe selfishness is the main reason for marital problems. Does it matter that people fill out their divorce petitions with words like irreconcilable differences, incompatibility, and financial trouble? In many cases the root problem is still just plain selfishness.

In counseling, I hear many complaints about lack of communication. Often one partner wants more conversation in the marriage. The other spouse doesn't like to talk or simply refuses to talk. What is that called? Selfishness.

Problems also occur when one partner is selfish when it comes to sexual pleasure. It isn't always deliberate or purposeful. Men are generally stimulated much faster than women. If a man doesn't realize (and his wife is too shy to tell him) that it takes a woman longer to become sexually aroused, he might hurry through the love-making process, reaching satisfaction while leaving his wife unfulfilled. He may not mean to be selfish, but if he doesn't learn to spend the necessary time caressing his wife, she may be deprived of sexual fulfillment.

When a woman is sexually deprived, she can become vulnerable in many ways. She may not ever intend to be unfaithful. But there is something subtle, something achingly lonely about a woman who is unfulfilled, that other men seem to sense. If the situation continues unchanged, one day, at her workplace or out in the world, someone may take advantage of the sexual dysfunction in her life, and everyone in the family will suffer.

People can also be very selfish in the ways they handle money. I have known women who charged their credit cards to the limit and created a financial burden on their households. That's selfishness. I have also known men who caused financial problems by spending ridiculous amounts of money playing golf, going to sporting events, or going hunting and fishing. It is selfish to spend money on personal satisfaction that should have been used to meet the needs of the entire family.

There are problems at the other end of the spectrum, too. I have heard from both men and women who say their spouses put them on such a meager allowance that they are sometimes forced to go without lunch and often have to borrow money just to make a phone call. That is humiliating, and it comes directly from selfishness.

Issues of Control

Selfishness is a control issue. A selfish husband and father may try to maintain control over his family by doling out small amounts of money so that they have to return often, subjecting themselves to him as they plead for more. In the same way, women who spend wildly and in an uncontrolled manner may be trying to control their husbands by keeping the family crippled by debt.

Healthy marriages are an open environment where both partners discuss their feelings, emotions and needs, and feel comfortable enough with each other to reveal the things that trouble them. Once problems arise, if either one feels insecure about discussing the situation, it may be a very strong indicator that the marriage is headed for trouble.

Unchecked stubbornness, selfishness, and control all have the power to sabotage a marriage. Husbands and wives need to make it a regular practice to discuss how they are going to spend money, what they are going to buy, and which items will best benefit the entire family. They should enjoy life and have fun. But any time one partner spends all the money or insists that his or her needs be met first, that is a danger sign.

Selfishness is listed in Galatians as a "work of the flesh." Look at what the Amplified Bible says, *"Now the doings (practices) of the flesh are clear (obvious): they are...selfishness..."* Galatians 5: 19-20, Amplified.

Selfishness is something to avoid and resist. In fact, God commands that we walk in love toward others, and part of walking in love is resisting selfishness (Ephesians 5: 2).

In the Book of First Corinthians, God gives us a description of the kind of love we are to have. *"Love (God's love in us) does not insist on its own rights or its own way, for it is not self-seeking..."* 1 Corinthians 13: 5, Amplified.

Selfishness makes people insist on their own rights and their own ways. It doesn't care who will be hurt or abused as long as the selfish desire gets satisfied. In a sense, selfishness is no respecter of persons. A selfish person will seek to be gratified, regardless of who gets hurt in the process. That includes children, a spouse, parents or anyone else who gets in the way.

When selfishness enters a marriage, the devil has a license to come into that home—even though the Bible warns us never to give the devil an open door or an opportunity to enter our lives. *"Leave no (such) room or foothold for the devil (give not opportunity to him)"* Ephesians 4: 27, Amplified. It is extremely important to resist selfishness in all areas of life, especially in marriage.

Stubbornness and selfishness are two factors that cause a multitude of marital problems. Primarily, they have to do with a person's tendency to yield to the flesh. Now let's take a look at some of the ways the devil makes active assaults on marriages.

The Enemy's Goal

The enemy will try to create strife and division in every family. His goals are physical and emotional abuse, adultery, and divorce, just to name a few. Sometimes I think he doesn't care if the marriage actually ends—as long as both partners are yelling and screaming, living in misery, and dreading each new day. He is very subtle. In many cases, his attacks go unnoticed. However, the results of these attacks are easy to recognize.

The devil can destroy a Christian marriage if the couple fails to realize that he is a deceiver. *"And the great dragon was cast out, that old serpent, called the Devil, and Satan. Which deceiveth the whole world..."* Revelation 12: 9.

Satan and God actually have something in common. That might shake some people, so let me explain. The Bible says God is no respecter of persons (Acts 10: 34). If God blesses one of His children, He is obligated to bless all of His children. The devil also is no respecter of persons, but in a much different way. He doesn't care if people are believers or non-believers. He doesn't care if they are rich or poor, young or old. He will attack anyone and any marriage. Now understand, I did not say God and Satan are alike in all areas, for we know God and the devil have totally different natures. God is light, but the devil is darkness. God is holy, but the devil is unholy. God wants us to prosper, but the devil wants us poor. God desires and has made provision for our success, while the devil tries daily to prevent that divine plan.

"For I know the plans I have for you, declares the Lord, plans to prosper you and not to harm you, plans to give you hope and a future" Jeremiah 29:11, NIV. God wants to prosper us and give us hope and a future in all areas of our lives. He desires that we thrive financially, spiritually, physically, and He also wants our marriages to prosper. He literally designed marriage to be *heaven on earth.*

"...Satan has desired to have you, that he may sift you as wheat" Luke 22:31. Satan wants to destroy our hope and wreck our futures, especially when it comes to marriage. Jesus told Peter that Satan wanted to sift him like wheat. What does that mean? When you sift wheat, you separate it. Jesus was literally telling Peter that Satan wanted to separate him from God.

Now if Satan wanted to separate Peter from God, you can be certain he has that same desire for you. And he won't stop there. He also wants to separate you from everything God promised you in the Word. He wants to separate you from financial prosperity, health, and your marriage partner. One of the chief tools he will use as he tries to accomplish that goal is *deception.*

The Power of Deception

How does the devil use deception to destroy marriages? There are several tricks he likes to play on unsuspecting victims. For example, Satan wants to convince each marriage partner that the other will never change. He will try to make them believe they are doomed to spend the rest of their lives in misery if they do not file for divorce. He also sets up temptations and opportunities for adultery. "No one will ever know," he says. "The grass is greener over there." He is a master at convincing people their spouses no longer love them. And when all else fails, he tries to deceive them into thinking they married the wrong person.

Each of these things is a lie straight from the pit of hell. The devil is a master of deception. He takes full advantage when people find themselves in a troubled marriage, and he uses their lack of faith and spiritual perception as a tool to destroy their marriage.

Satan longs to devour you! I think there is a lot of confusion in the world about this fact. People like to think they are too sophisticated to believe in an actual hell that houses an actual devil. But watch them all flock to the latest demonic offering from Hollywood or gravitate to articles about ghosts and hauntings in the tabloids. On the one hand, people say they do not believe in the devil, but on the other hand, they continually prove that they do. And that devil is out to steal their eternity! The Word says, *"Be sober, be vigilant; because your adversary the devil, as a roaring lion, walketh about, seeking whom he may devour: Whom resist steadfast in the faith, knowing that the same afflictions are accomplished in your brethren that are in the world"* 1 Peter 5: 8-9, KJV.

It's Our Responsibility

Notice that God gives the final responsibility to us. He tells us to be sober and alert and to watch out for the tricks the enemy will pull. I wonder how many marriages might be saved if husbands and wives made sure they heeded that verse, if they stayed ever alert for the enemy's attacks. It is our responsibility to protect our marriages and our marriage partners from assaults on the family's health, finances, and children. Spiritual growth is vital, and it helps us recognize and defeat these attacks.

Satan's power is limited. Unfortunately, even many Christians seem to forget that. Look at the simple wording of 1 Peter 5:8, *"Be sober, be vigilant; because your adversary the devil walks about like a roaring lion, seeking whom he may devour."* <u>Whom he may!</u> He can devour only *certain* people and *certain* marriages. He is not all-powerful, nor can he control a child of God who recognizes him and resists his attacks. He has to have permission. Who gives him that permission?

We do when we make the kinds of choices that give him entry into our lives.

Sometimes people are not totally to blame for the choices they make. Hosea 4:6 says, *"My people are destroyed for lack of knowledge."* Satan is able to destroy those who are ignorant of God's Word. Did you know that God tells husbands to get knowledge concerning their wives? *"Likewise, ye husbands, dwell with them according to knowledge..."* 1 Peter 3:7. I think one reason God instructed husbands this way is because He knew men would need a lot of knowledge to understand women. (Some men have even given up hope of ever gaining this wisdom!) Through a man's eyes, women *can* be hard to understand. Many current books take advantage of this confusion and exploit the frustration felt by both sexes.

God understands the devil works best when there is a lack of knowledge. Satan, as well as most of the secular world, does not want people to make an effort to gain this knowledge. If husbands and wives would educate themselves about each other, they could effectively close the door on the enemy in many areas. With each bit of knowledge you gain about your spouse, you lower the chances of having a misunderstanding.

I am so tired of seeing the devil destroy marriages! I believe the Word of God can set us free from the tricks of the enemy. When people learn to watch for and resist Satan's attacks, he loses power in their lives and in their marriages. The Bible says we have authority over all the forces of evil. However, we must use that authority to benefit from it.

"I have given you authority to trample on snakes and scorpions and to overcome all the power of the enemy; nothing will harm you" Luke 10:19, NIV.

God has given us the strength and wisdom to stop the devil from causing strife in our homes. He has given us all the power we need to resist our flesh. But it is our choice, just as the people of Israel had a choice when God talked about the blessings and the curses in Deuteronomy 28.

We will all face situations in our marriages—opportunities where we have to choose to either follow our flesh (selfishness, stubbornness, infidelity) or walk in love. Our decisions determine the degree of happiness and fulfillment we will find in marriage.

The Results of Poor Choices

One of the saddest things I have observed in my church and others, is the high numbers of older single women. What a tragedy to see so many women alone in their golden years. These women, who often gave their youth to childbearing, housekeeping, the struggles of putting a young husband through college or helping him climb a corporate ladder, often find themselves cast aside once the husband achieves success. Why is this?

Certainly it reflects selfishness and poor choices.

But maybe it isn't as one-sided as it looks. Often, as husbands make their way through the maze of career moves and adjustments, wives learn to get by on their own. They get jobs. They get involved in volunteer work, politics, or recreations like bowling, cards, or golf. They throw themselves into their children's activities and educational goals.

The marriage becomes routine; it shifts into a rut. Spouses begin to pass each other briefly as they shuttle back and forth between work, hobbies, sporting events, and the activities they have invented to fill the terrible void left by the honey that ran freely from their honeymoon!

I try to imagine these couples on those rare occasions when they are home on the same night, at the same time, when they actually go to bed together. What do they say? How do they feel? How do they deal with the aching loneliness as they face the reality that they are growing further and further apart?

If the devil has his way, this is when the blaming, shaming, and nagging begin. He says/she says. They try to cover the ripping pain of lost love with the importance of jobs, the necessity of volunteer work, the significance of Little League, ballet, after-school projects, and high school athletics—and, of course, the validity of the choices they have made. Rather than confront their loss, knocking down the walls that have risen between them, the couple begins to justify their individual behaviors.

In their pain, in their deep sense of rejection and failure, they roll away from each other when their only hope was in reaching out, taking comfort in each other's arms, and rekindling the love that once made them a couple. Stony silence and bitter tears fill the void, neither of them hearing the devil's cackles of delight as the curtain comes down on their marriage.

Maybe they stay together for the kids. Some couples do. But the rejection and pain in their bedroom often drives one or both of them into the arms of other people. Eventually the children leave home. By that time, the husband and wife are strangers. One or the other finally leaves. Any semblance of equality of the sexes ends there.

There are many more middle-aged women than men. And many young women like the idea of marrying an older man who is established in his career and financially comfortable. Inevitably, some of these divorced men marry younger women. These relationships are good for their egos—egos that have been ignored, deflated, and hungry for years.

But the children from the first marriage may feel alienated. They do not want to end up in the middle of their parents' cold war. They don't like watching their father bounce a happy, spoiled toddler on his knee when all they can remember is that he was too busy to take an active role in their lives when they were young.

And the first wife? She seems to pay the highest price. She spends her golden years alone, perhaps going out for an occasional dinner with friends, working at a job that rarely pays the kind of salary she would get if she hadn't spent twenty years or more raising children at home.

There are too many costs to count in this familiar scenario. Retirement funds are usually broken up, most of their value lost. The golden years that a couple once planned to enjoy become additional working years. Children lose the easy familiarity they should have with both parents. Older husbands may find themselves exhausted, trying to keep up with their young wives and young families.

The first wife, now alone, bitter and angry, struggles to heal. Both original spouses feel the pain of failure and regret, wondering how different their retirement years might have been if they had persevered more, tried harder, and made different choices. How would their lives have been if they had only guarded the honey in their honeymoon more carefully?

This scenario is not rare in today's society! It is frighteningly common. There are no winners. Well, only one—Satan. This is what he wanted all along. If you see yourself heading down this path, it is my deepest desire that you will be able to pull back. Joel 2:25 says, *"Then I will make up to you for the years that the swarming locust has eaten, the creeping locust, the stripping locust, and the gnawing locust...."*

What does that Scripture mean? It means *it is never too late with God*! He will restore the years the locust ate! He will give back to us the joy of our youth, the promise of our marriage vows, the comfort, pleasure and respect of the 'friend' we married. It is a matter of choice. It will require great sacrifice, including the laying down of selfish patterns, pride and a willful nature.

But the rewards will be enormous. Of all the honey in the honeymoon, the aged honey is the best! It is worth waiting for, working for, and making many sacrifices to find.

"So I say, live by the Spirit, and you will not gratify the desires of the sinful nature" Galatians 5: 16. We have been commanded to walk in the spirit and not fulfill the lust of the flesh. God knows this will save us a lot of heartache. It will provide a safe, healthy, and tranquil home where children thrive, and where they work to be all they can be in the Lord.

Be alert to Satan's attacks against marriage. He does not want any marriage to succeed. Resist him in the name of Jesus!

Chapter 3

Don't Settle for Less

God made wonderful plans for our lives and our marriages. That's the truth. People are the ones who changed the reality. When we look at the world today with its out-of-control divorce rates, the huge numbers of infants born out of wedlock, high-profile stories of physical and emotional abuse, and the casual attitudes reflected on television and in movies regarding marriage and committed relationships, it is difficult to remember that God's plan was different.

"So commit yourselves completely to these words of mine. Tie them to your hands as a reminder, and wear them on your forehead. ...so that as long as the sky remains above the earth, you and your children may flourish in the land the Lord swore to give to your ancestors" Deuteronomy 11: 18, 21, TLB.

He wants us to have days of heaven on earth. He wants us to have the same kind of life He lives in heaven. What kind of life is that? According to the Word, it's wonderful. There is no poverty nor sickness in heaven. There is no strife and no division. When God created man, He wanted us to enjoy all those benefits right here on earth. God wants us to have heaven on earth in our marriages.

The institution of marriage was God's idea. As soon as He created man, He created woman. *"And the LORD God said, 'It is not good that man should be alone; I will make him a helper comparable to him'"* Genesis 2: 18. So God caused a deep sleep to fall on Adam, and He took one of his ribs and formed Eve.

He designed us to love, need, compliment, and balance each other. Where one was weak, He made the other strong. He designed men to be tough enough to fight off threats, to hunt and provide food for their families. Read the Old Testament. Life was not easy once Adam and Eve were evicted from the Garden of Eden. Men had to be fast, and often fierce.

God balanced women with more tender natures, with compassion and empathy and tears. Not only did they need this gentleness for nurturing children, but also to comfort and relax their husbands after a punishing day.

God's original intent for marriage was for it to be a source of intimate fellowship, joy and happiness. Adam and Eve were to dwell together in a state of oneness, enjoying each other and the life they had. That was God's original plan, and it is still His plan today.

God never intended for marriage to be a source of pain, resentment, and agony. However, some people do experience it that way because they have failed to learn how to do things God's way. We cannot expect God's best without knowing and following His Word.

John and I have always believed God wanted our marriage to be sweet. We knew from reading the Scriptures that His desire was for us to have a loving and mutually satisfying marriage. But even though that was God's plan, it didn't just happen. We also had to *know* it was God's will. We had to *understand* what God intended for our lives. Before you can believe for any promise in the Word, you must be sure it is God's will. After you get the mind of Christ on a situation, then you can properly release your faith.

I want to encourage you to study and practice the principles in this chapter. The next few pages can make a good marriage better, and a bad marriage good. Regardless of past mistakes, God is ready to restore the honey you have lost from your honeymoon. However, before He can begin to work in your marriage, you must realize your situation is subject to change.

God Can Heal Any Marriage

Never forget that God can change a person's heart overnight. A praying wife can go to bed with a grizzly bear and wake up next to a teddy bear. That is the absolute truth. I have witnessed many men and women change through the power of God in a short period of time.

The Scriptures clearly prove this point. Saul of Tarsus is a good example. He was once a murderer, and his goal in life was to destroy Christianity. If God can transform a man like Saul from a murderer into a man of God, think what He can do with a grumpy or non-communicative spouse.

Once we realize God can change people and marriages, the question becomes, how will these changes occur? There are only two ways—through prayer and by doing the Word. If you have been waiting many years for your spouse to change, I have a word from the Lord!

Don't give up!

God has promised days of heaven on earth, and the Word of God declares that He is faithful to perform His promises (Hebrews 10:23). If you stand fast on the Word of God, you will see a change. On the other hand, if you try to change your spouse through your own strength, you will ultimately fail. Notice what else the Word of God says. *"...Not by might, nor by power, but by my spirit, says the Lord of hosts"* Zechariah 4:6.

We could paraphrase that scripture to say, "Not by whining, nor by nagging...." There are a lot of jokes in the secular world about women and their tendency to nag, and those jokes are not totally without merit. Women are different from men. They receive and process information differently. What a man considers nagging from a woman is usually just her way of communicating her concerns. Sometimes she thinks he hasn't heard her or that maybe he didn't understand what she was saying.

Men, on the other hand, have a tendency to block out those things they do not wish to hear or that they cannot change or deal with right at that moment. It is no surprise that these two ways of handling the issues come into conflict.

Just as ignoring a wife is not the proper way to deal with a situation, neither is it correct to nag. Many couples develop the following destructive pattern: She talks, he ignores; she complains, he ignores; she threatens, he ignores. That pattern leads to trouble. In fact, it is one of the fastest ways to damage a marriage, often to the point that the honey begins to pour out onto the ground.

When things are not as a wife would like them—let's say her husband refuses to go to church—and she understands that talking, complaining and threatening won't work, what should she do? Pray. God will hear. The Word says, "*...and if your people offer a prayer concerning their troubles or sorrow, raising their hands toward this Temple, then hear from heaven where you live, and forgive. Give your people whatever they deserve, for you alone know the human heart*" 1 Kings 8: 38-39, TLB.

From the counseling I have done over the years, I now realize that many times people try to inflict change on a spouse instead of letting God deal with the situation. Yet the Word is clear, "*Casting the whole of your care [all your anxieties, all your worries, all your concerns, once and for all] on Him, for He cares for you affectionately and cares about you watchfully*" 1 Peter 5:7, Amplified.

We are supposed to cast all our anxieties, worries and concerns on the Lord. What does *all* mean? It simply means each and every problem, worry, or fear. Some people cast their financial concerns on the Lord, but hang on to their marital worries. When they do that, God is free to bless them in financial areas, but He will still wait for permission before addressing their marital problems.

When people choose to obey the Word and cast their cares on the Lord, they literally give God an opportunity to work in their lives. That's good. Because no matter how hard you try, you will never change your spouse by fleshly means. It takes revelation from God to bring about permanent change and healing. Complaining and nagging will never get the job done.

In order to bless us in this area, God has given instruction on how to encourage change in a spouse. *"In the same way, you wives must accept the authority of your husbands, even those who refuse to accept the Good News. Your godly lives will speak to them better than any words. They will be won over by watching your pure, godly behavior"* 1 Peter 3:1-2, TLB.

This Scripture reveals important information. Actions speak louder than words. When a wife has a husband who refuses to go to church with her, she should not begin to *instruct* him in godly ways, or *tell* him all the wonderful things the men at church say and do for their wives. That will not have a positive affect. The Scripture says godly *lives* and pure, godly *behavior* will win such husbands over! This may be revelation for some people.

For those who prefer the King James Version of this Scripture, let's look at it. *"Likewise, ye wives, be in subjection to your own husbands; that, if any obey not the word, they also may without the word be won by the conversation of the wives; While they behold your chaste conversation coupled with fear."* Conversation sounds like *talking*. But the Greek definition of conversation, according to Strong's Concordance, is *behavior*. That agrees with The Living Bible. Husbands are not won by the words of their wives, but rather by their behavior and conduct.

I have known women who refused to make love to their husbands unless they agreed to go to church with them. No wonder so many men are bitter toward the church. These women were manipulating their husbands. What kind of example is that? An unbelieving husband will automatically think the church is behind his wife's neglect in taking care of his physical needs. To the unrenewed man, this kind of attitude indicates that his wife's church is nothing more than a place of torment.

When a husband refuses to go to church or to do what is right, his wife should not withhold sex from him. In fact, she should make love to him as if there is no conflict. Afterward, she should invite him to go to church! He might not go at first, but at least his wife is obeying God's principles, and when she does that, she has every right to expect God to move on her behalf.

Prayer is also important. I'm sure you already know you should pray for your spouse. However, it is not just a matter of knowing it, but doing it. It becomes much easier to nag and complain than it is to pray. Since the results of prayer are usually not seen immediately, some people would rather rely on the flesh. This is a dangerous situation because nagging will only cause additional problems. Prayer, on the other hand, has the ability to change the other person. This is what the Bible says about the effectiveness of prayer:

"*...The earnest (heartfelt, continued) prayer of a righteous man [or woman] makes tremendous power available [dynamic in its working]* James 5:16, Amplified.

Praise God! The Word of God says tremendous power is available when we pray. Many people have faith in the prayer of their pastor, but no faith in their own prayers. That is wrong. Every righteous person's earnest and heartfelt prayers have power! And that power can transform your spouse or any situation. It can bring about life-altering change. We know what the Word says about prayer, so the question becomes: will you spend the necessary time in prayer to see your spouse changed forever?

I want to point out one key word from that Scripture. "*...The earnest (heartfelt, continued) prayer of a righteous man [or woman] makes tremendous power available [dynamic in its working]*. A key word here is *continued*. What does *continued* mean? It means once you have chosen to stand in the gap for your spouse, you should persist in your prayers. Unfortunately, it's in the area of persistence where many people give up.

In the name of Jesus, don't give up! Continue to pray, even when it seems there is no visible change. Remember, "*...faith is the substance of things hoped for and the evidence of things not seen*" Hebrews 11:1.

The Bible is full of examples of people who would not let go of God's Word, even in the face of perceived defeat. David believed in God despite the giant he was about to face, and God gave him the victory (1 Samuel 17). Abraham trusted God in the face of contrary evidence, and he became the father of many nations (*Romans 4:18-21*).

Joshua and the children of Israel shouted before they ever saw the walls of Jericho fall (*Joshua 6:1-20*).

When we make the choice to persist in faith and prayer, God can change situations.

We possess that which we confess. There is a lot of truth in that old saying. If you declare your spouse is no good, he or she will be no good. If you constantly tell others you have an awful spouse (even if that is the truth), you will continue to experience an awful spouse. On the other hand, if you profess you are married to a godly man or woman, God can and will move on your behalf. The Word of God clearly reveals that the things we believe and confess will come to pass.

The subject of confession is not the focus of this book, but I do want to share a few scriptures that explain how the words we say can affect both life and marriage.

"...Whoever shall say unto this mountain, Be thou removed, and be thou cast into the sea; and shall not doubt in his heart, but shall believe that those things which he saith shall come to pass; he shall have whatever he saith" Mark 11:23b, KJV.

"A wholesome tongue is a tree of life." Proverbs 15:4, KJV.

"Death and life are in the power of the tongue: and they that love it shall eat the fruit thereof" Proverbs 18:21, KJV.

We can see from these scriptures that the words we say are very important. We need to ask ourselves, "Are we confessing good things or bad things concerning our marriages?"

Sometimes when women get together, the topic of conversation turns to their mates. It is not uncommon to hear, "My husband is terrible." Or "My husband doesn't care about me anymore." When a woman speaks that way about her husband and she is sincerely seeking prayer or advice, it might be all right. But be careful! If such conversation is a tactic to get sympathy or attention from friends, it will only increase your problems at home. We will never see any change for the better until we stop speaking those kinds of words. Negative words have the power to shoot destructive arrows into our marriages, ripping deep holes that let the honey trickle out.

Romans 4:17 says, *"As it is written: 'I have made you a father of many nations.' He is our father in the sight of God, in whom he believed—the God who gives life to the dead and calls things that are not as though they were"* NIV. We need to remember that. We need to begin to thank God for spouses that are changing daily. Praise God that your spouse is becoming the mighty man or woman He designed them to be. I encourage you to get up every morning, lift your hands to heaven and say, "Thank You, Father God, that my spouse is a Christian. He is delivered from the kingdom of darkness and is walking in the light of Your Word. My spouse is a man of God who loves me and our children. He is growing daily in the knowledge of God. Thank You, Lord, that the Holy Ghost is transforming him into the image of Jesus Christ."

At noon, confess the Word again. And again at bedtime. Thank God for His Word and thank Him in advance for the answer to that prayer.

While I used the illustration of a wife confessing the Word over her husband, there are many husbands who should be confessing the Word over their wives. We need to learn to confess the things we want to see manifested in our spouses. I am not talking about confessing that a spouse will run out and buy you a diamond ring or a new set of golf clubs. That is not faith—it is spiritual manipulation. I am talking about confessing the things the Word of God says about His people. For example, the Word of God says, *"...the love of God is shed abroad in our hearts by the Holy Ghost..."* Romans 5:5. Therefore, if you want your spouse to be more loving, thank God for that love being manifested in a greater measure.

It is important that we never give up praying and confessing the Word. The devil will try to distract us and attack our faith. He'll say, "It's not working," or "This will never change." Don't listen to his lies. Resist the thoughts of the enemy and hold fast to the confession of faith.

"Let us hold fast the profession of our faith without wavering; (for he is

faithful that promised)" Hebrews 10:23, KJV.

The word *profession* actually means *confession*. We are to hold fast to the confession of our faith. Why? Because the devil will try to steal it! Don't let that happen. Don't let him steal God's best, the things He has planned and designed for all of us. Stand firm and confess the Word. Because, "*...He is faithful that promised*" Hebrews 10:23. Remember that God has promised us days of heaven on earth, and that includes the days while we are married. Refuse to waiver. Hold fast the confession of faith. God will bring His Word to pass.

Living the Word, praying the Word, and confessing the Word every day are the three most powerful ways to affect change in your marriage. Each step comes directly from the Bible.

Where Should We Turn for Help?

When we need advice, psychologists, counselors, relatives, and friends are helpful only if they base their advice on the Word of God. Much of the counsel given by unbelievers is both unreliable and unscriptural. For example, there was a time when I was ill, and a doctor advised me to have an affair in order to get well. Obviously, that was ungodly and unscriptural counsel! Resist that kind of guidance—just as I did.

I instantly recognized that doctor's advice as bad, but many well-meaning people may give unscriptural counsel. Every piece of advice should be judged according to the Word of God. Does it agree with the Bible? Does it promote and show the love of God? If not, reject it. Only the advice based on the Word will lead to godly and fulfilling Christian marriages.

Revenge, threats, and a "get-even" mentality will never work. I don't care what anybody else has said. When people resort to advice that is contrary to the Word, they tie God's hands. He will be unable to move on your behalf if you choose to live in disobedience to His divine will.

If you have already made the mistake, don't be discouraged. Don't give up. It is not too late to change. We must get our thinking lined up with God's Word. He has solutions for all marital problems. Study the Word and *apply* its wisdom.

Apply is an active word. It means we have to do something. I have pastored people for a very long time, and nearly every week someone comes to me and asks for prayer for their marriage. Most just want me to pray a nice little prayer, lay my hands on them, and make their marriages wonderful again.

There is a problem with that kind of thinking. We all know prayer works, but prayer is not a spiritual pardon that releases people from the responsibility of being *doers of the Word*. Many people have failed to study the Word, and even more have failed to be doers of the Word when it comes to their marriages. Straightening out a marriage relationship, undoing years of game playing, manipulation, abuse, dysfunction, or stubbornness, takes more than a prayer. The people involved *must* become doers of the Word, reading and understanding the things God expects, overcoming habits and negative patterns, laying down their lives so they might see miraculous changes occur.

"*...whoso looketh into the perfect law of liberty, and continueth therein, he being not a forgetful hearer, but a doer of the work, this man shall be blessed in his deed*" James 1:25, KJV.

God is not a respecter of persons. He is not a man that He should lie. All of this power, grace, and favor is available to everyone. But we have to act. We have to stretch. We have to realize that continuing in our old ways, our habits, our comfortable ruts and patterns will not bring change. There is a famous saying, "Insanity is doing the same things over and over again and expecting different results." That is so true! Asking someone to pray over a spouse or a critical family situation is a waste of time if we refuse to change or do anything about the situation.

Be a doer of the Word! Throughout the scriptures, God promised to deliver those who put the Word first and agreed to do what it said. Here are a few examples:

"...If you fully obey the LORD your God and carefully follow all his commands I give you today, the LORD your God will set you high above all the nations on earth. All these blessings will come upon you and accompany you if you obey the LORD your God" Deuteronomy 28:1-2, NIV.

"See, I am setting before you today a blessing and a curse—the blessing if you obey the commands of the LORD your God that I am giving you today" Deuteronomy 11:26-27, NIV.

"...Blessed are they that hear the Word of God, and keep it" Luke 11:28b, KJV.

We can clearly see that doers of the Word experience God's best. Be a doer. Obey the Word and live a godly life. Pray and confess the Word of God. God wants you to experience your marriages as heaven on earth. He wants your mate to bring you joy, peace, and fulfillment. But you must obey His Word in order to receive His best.

Chapter 4

Biblical Order in the Home

God has designed a proper order for the home. When I use the term *proper order,* I mean God has a specific place where each member of the family should function. The husband should understand his position and how it relates to his wife and children. The wife should understand her position and how it relates to the rest of the family. And finally, the children should understand their position and how it relates to the mother and father.

Proper order establishes authority in the home. Who is the head of the family? Who makes the final decisions? Who is responsible for leading the family? Since God's Word addresses proper order in the home, we should recognize its importance and strive to maintain it in our families.

Will people always understand biblical order? Absolutely not—especially if they are unchurched or unsaved. Many times, co-workers, family members, or well-meaning friends will criticize couples that choose to run their homes using the principles of biblical order. If you get that kind of interference, you need to ask yourself a few questions: Does God's way work? Do godly children prosper, excel, and develop into high-functioning adults? Do godly husbands and wives thrive in their relationship? Will you choose to please God or the world?

The fruit of secular marriage is obvious. Divorce rates have spiraled out of control. There is often a constant and bitter struggle for power between worldly husbands and wives. Hundreds of thousands of children are growing up with stepparents, often the second or third such arrangement they have experienced. Many of these children have anger issues, and they are acting out with drugs, promiscuity, and rebellion.

In other words, the world's marriage system isn't working. So why should we care what they think about our efforts to do it God's way? God has a plan! It works. If you follow His plan, it will cover your family with security, solid values, and a sense of order and accomplishment.

God's commands to His people are not simply requests. He expects us to do what His Word says. Families who are seeking a way out of dysfunction, financial problems, and many other challenges must learn to obey God's Word. *"And whatsoever we ask, we receive of Him, because we keep His commandments, and do those things that are pleasing in His sight"* 1 John 3:22, NKJV.

Why do we receive what we ask? *"...because we keep His commandments, and do those things that are pleasing in His sight."* That seems to say that some people *fail* to receive because they refuse to, *"...keep His commandments, and do those things that are pleasing in His sight."* If you are wondering why God never seems to answer your prayers, ask yourself, "Am I keeping God's commandments?" A failure to obey the Word can hinder God's ability to move in your life.

Those who fail to adhere to God's biblical order for their homes, are limiting Him. Remember, our God is a gentleman. He will never intrude in areas where we have not given our consent.

God's Order

God gave the husband the responsibility of being the head of the family. (1 Corinthians 11:3) If homes are to be happy and well ordered, husbands and wives must get into agreement regarding this basic principle of the Word. Just because the Bible says the husband is to be the head of the home, does it give him the right to be a tyrant, to be unfair, cruel or selfish? Absolutely not. In fact, a husband who lives under biblical order will be just the opposite. He will be loving to his wife, a good provider, a tender, caring father, and he will bless his family with an inheritance. (Ephesians 5)

I believe God intended for us to leave a financial inheritance to our children, but just as important, we are to leave our children an inheritance of integrity, good stewardship, and honor. Some people verbally consent to the Word, but fail to obey it. If you want to enjoy the fruit of a Christian family, be willing to do *all* that God commands in His Word.

Embracing Christian Values

There is support for husbands who want to take a proper role in their families. I think a good example is Promise Keepers. I've never been to a Promise Keeper's meeting, but I've seen their fruit. Men who get involved with that organization and go to their events, seem committed to being strong, loving and generous family leaders. I'm saddened when I hear society attack them. Should we throw out Promise Keepers because their organization is for men only?

When did we, as a society, get to be such bullies? No group, not Christians, not the secular world, not even the government—has the right to *force* their opinions and their lifestyles on everyone else. I marvel at the people—women included—who still run around with their militant placards and their harsh voices. They protest everything from Promise Keepers to albacore tuna. Meanwhile, in many of the Christian homes they scorn, wives are enjoying attentive, doting husbands, children are doing their homework and getting good grades, bills are paid and there's money in the bank. Is it any wonder that God said, *"...people are destroyed for lack of knowledge"* Hosea 4:6, NKJV.

What benefit will a woman ultimately gain if she insists on being the head of her family, and that family ends up in divorce—with family members splintered, bitter and lost? When a wife tries to usurp her husband's authority, problems manifest quickly. The Christian family can be such a wonderful institution if every member understands proper order, but it will not work if the wife decides to take the leadership from her husband. Some women have very forceful personalities and tend to be more aggressive than their husbands. This can be a good thing—a part of the balance God set into that particular marriage. Just remember, her strengths do not give her authority to take over the leadership of the home.

This order is so easy for the world to misunderstand, and it's often a stumbling block for Christian women. But it shouldn't be. We are not talking about men being dictators or making decisions without talking things over with their wives. Why would God tell a couple to get into *agreement* on issues if He didn't expect them to sometimes have differing opinions? When a compromise can't be reached, when a decision has to be made, but there is still confusion about the proper course or choice, I think of the "head of he family" as the person who must take responsibility for making that decision. That's not necessarily a cushy job or a prestigious position. If that judgment turns out to be wrong, who takes the blame?

Ultimately, someone has to make final decisions. Otherwise, when those situations arise, families will spend all their time stuck in uncertainty. Husbands and wives need to thoroughly discuss their options. They also need to pray for guidance . But when prayer and discussion fail to bring clarity, the husband is the one who should make the final decision. Personally, when that task falls to John, I breathe a sigh of relief. I don't want the weight of all our family decisions. I don't want to be responsible for making the wrong choice. And I certainly don't feel cheated because I don't have that liability.

Husbands are also responsible for guiding the spiritual lives of their families. For those who might not think this is true, just take a look at friends and family members. Where a husband's heart is turned to the Lord, families pray before meals, they tithe and give offerings, attend church regularly, and live lives committed to service in the Kingdom. In homes where the husband is not saved and does not honor the Father, audible prayers are more rare, tithes and offerings tend to be lower, and church attendance is often more sporadic.

I do think churches could reach out in a more effective manner, that they could show more compassion for families that come from homes where the husband and father is unsaved. We need to support and love these women, pray for them, and help them in the task of raising godly children.

In a Christian family, Jesus Christ is manifest in the home. He lives there. His presence is real, felt and tangible. The people in that home try to live like Jesus, think like Jesus, and treat others as Jesus would treat them if He still lived on earth. Jesus is the example we should all work to emulate.

Living in the Presence of Jesus

There are two keys to developing a family's relationship with Jesus. First, all family members should realize they are living in the presence of the Lord. What do I mean by that? They should realize that Jesus lives in each one of them, so He is present all the time. He doesn't just see us at church. He sees us on the highway. He sees us when we are standing in lines at the bank or the grocery store. He knows when the words we say at church do not line up with the actions we display out in the world. He sees us in our homes. He sees the way we behave. Are we fair? Are we righteous? Do we take out our frustrations on the ones who love us the most?

It is amazing how some people act once they leave church. As a pastor, I encounter this too often. Some of the nicest, sweetest and most spiritual people on Sunday can turn out to be quite different on Monday. Some of them tell dirty jokes and use profanity with their friends at work. Others gossip or display tremendous anger and disrespect to people in stores and restaurants. Still others are profane and abusive when they drive. Some give stingy tips to waiters and waitresses or act rude to people in their workplace. Why do they bother acting nice in my presence? Are they showing me respect? The truth is, they should respect Jesus much more than me, and He is always watching. The Bible says He will never leave us or forsake us (Hebrews 13:5). This means He sees our behavior at church, at work, at home, and everywhere we go.

It is obvious that some people fail to realize that Jesus is living in their home. They curse, slam doors, kick things around, and knock holes in the walls. I can't help but believe this would change if people honestly understood they had a guest named Jesus Christ watching every action, hearing every word.

Whenever Jesus is truly Lord of our homes, we won't push our ways over His ways. We will think, act and speak as He would—especially in our homes. We need to make it a habit to ask, when we're confronted with challenging situations, "What would Jesus want me to do? How would Jesus act in this situation?"

Understanding Divine Order

The second key to developing a Christian family is understanding the divine order we've been discussing. Christian families need to recognize and establish correct authority between various members. The Bible plainly declares the roles of husbands and wives.

Where does divine order begin? With Jesus! He should be the ultimate head of a home. "*...I would have you know, that the head of every man (husband) is Christ...*" 1 Corinthians 11:3, KJV. This verse says that Christ is the head of every husband. Since Christ is the head, then each man will have to give an account of how well he obeyed the Lord's instructions. In the natural realm, most of us have a boss at work. That boss expects us to obey his commands. If he says to type a letter, call someone, or make a sale, we're expected to do just that. The boss is over us (the head). He expects his orders to be followed.

The same thing is true in the Kingdom of God. Husbands are to obey Christ's commands. When they do, they are promised favor and blessings. Think of it this way: If you would obey your boss at work, how much more should you obey the King of Kings and the Lord of Lords?

"*...the head of every man is Christ; and the head of the woman is the man...*" 1 Corinthians 11:3, KJV. This is where the world likes to jump in and muddy the waters. But they're making a mistake. God's Word says that husbands are second in command. They are the chief authorities, after Christ, in their families. Although God has given men the headship of the home, that position comes with tremendous responsibility.

Some husbands get the idea that as the head, they don't have to give an account to anyone. That is simply not true. Husbands will give an account to the King of Kings for the way they have treated and led their families!

"...every one of us shall give account of himself to God" Romans 14:12, KJV. Some husbands may say, "I don't know how to lead my family. My wife has been a Christian for twenty-five years and I just got saved."

I was saved a lot longer than John, but he rose up and took his place as the head of our home. When a man decides to submit his life to Jesus, it seems the Lord puts him on an accelerated spiritual growth program. If a man truly wants to be all God designed him to be, God will help him. Husbands who feel inferior in spiritual matters shouldn't get confused or condemned because their wives may be more mature Christians. Godly wives will readily submit because one day they will also be called to give an account.

"Wives, submit yourselves unto your own husbands, as unto the Lord" Ephesians 5:22, KJV. P*ease* notice this verse says, *"...unto your own husbands."* That is clear teaching that women are not subject to, nor should they submit, to all men. Men are not superior to women. That's not what biblical order is all about.

Responsibilities of a Husband

So, husbands have the responsibility of being the heads of our homes. They must live in submission to Christ, make quality decisions, discipline the children, provide for the family, lead the family in spiritual matters, and be a source of security. This is not an easy job, but the Lord will help them every step of the way.

Did you know the Scriptures tell fathers to train their children? *"Fathers, do not exasperate your children; instead, bring them up in the training and instruction of the Lord"* Ephesians 6:4, NIV.

Traditionally, wives have been given the responsibility to train and discipline the children. However, the Word of God tells us fathers are to play a major role in this process. Husbands are responsible for teaching their children about spiritual things. Fathers should not just tell the children what to do; rather they should show them. That is done by principle and example. Children will learn to worship God when they see their parents worship God. When parents read the Bible, give tithes and offerings, love others and pray, they give their children a powerful lesson. The old expression, "Do what I say, not what I do," will not teach a child good habits.

Both parents need to set proper examples in front of their children. When they *know* the Word of God, it can become their lifestyle. That is the way children will learn to apply God's principles to their own lives.

Husbands also have the responsibility of providing for the family. *"But if any provide not for his own, and specially for those of his own house, he hath denied the faith, and is worse than an infidel"* 1 Timothy 5:8, KJV.

That is straight talk. It means husbands should work to supply the needs of their families. If they do not, they have, *"...denied the faith, and (are) worse than an infidel."* Why worse than an infidel? Because most unbelievers are decent enough to provide for their families.

Women in the Workforce

This does not mean that wives cannot assist their husbands. There are examples in the Word of women who helped supplement the family income. Do you remember the virtuous woman in Proverbs 31?

"Her husband has full confidence in her and lacks nothing of value. She brings him good, not harm, all the days of her life. She selects wool and flax

and works with eager hands. She is like the merchant ships, bringing her food from afar. She gets up while it is still dark; she provides food for her family and portions for her servant girls. She considers a field and buys it; out of her earnings she plants a vineyard. She sets about her work vigorously; her arms are strong for her tasks. She sees that her trading is profitable, and her lamp does not go out at night. In her hand she holds the distaff and grasps the spindle with her fingers. She opens her arms to the poor and extends her hands to the needy. When it snows, she has no fear for her household; for all of them are clothed in scarlet. She makes coverings for her bed; she is clothed in fine linen and purple. Her husband is respected at the city gate, where he takes his seat among the elders of the land. She makes linen garments and sells them, and supplies the merchants with sashes" Proverbs 31, NIV.

This woman was doing some serious work! We really have to honor and respect her. She was busy and hard-working. Notice she had love and respect from all the people around her. She was no doormat. Women have no reason to fear biblical order if that is an example of a godly woman.

There were times when I helped John supply for our family. When he was enrolled in Bible College, we had four small children, and our finances were very limited. I do mean *very* limited. John and I weren't looking for positions; we were looking for jobs! For a while he cleaned a restaurant and worked as a night watchman. He couldn't continue to do that and go to school. So I ironed people's clothes, babysat, and worked as a carhop. Together, we accomplished what we knew God wanted us to do.

Wives are referred to as helpmeets in Genesis 2:18. "*...And the LORD God said, It is not good that the man should be alone; I will make him a help meet...*" KJV. One of the ways to help your husband is by assisting financially. There may even be situations where wives make more money than their husbands. When that happens, he should not feel intimidated as long as he is working to supply for his family. But even though wives can assist, God has placed the primary responsibility of providing for their families on husbands.

What about love? Is it enough to just feed, clothe and teach? No. The Bible says, *"Husbands, love your wives, even as Christ also loved the church, and gave Himself for it"* Ephesians 5:25, KJV.

The King James Version of the Bible uses several different Greek words for the word *love*. One of them means "a friendship type love." Another means "sexual love." However, the one used in this verse is *agapao*, which is "the God-kind of love." This love is unconditional. It seeks and does what is best for others. That is the kind of love husbands are to have for their wives. A man should love his wife unconditionally—just as Christ loved the church. That is the deepest kind of love. Jesus loved the church so much that He literally gave His life for it. A husband may not die for his wife, but as he goes to work and provides for her and for his family, he is giving his life.

The Role of the Wife

God did not restrict his instructions to the men. He gave training to women as well. *"Likewise, teach the older women to be reverent in the way they live, not to be slanderers or addicted to much wine, but to teach what is good. Then they can train the younger women to love their husbands and children, to be self-controlled and pure, to be busy at home, to be kind, and to be subject to their husbands, so that no one will malign* [smear] *the word of God"* Titus 2:3-5, NIV.

In the book of Titus, the Apostle Paul gives instructions for older and younger women. First he addresses the older because they have a responsibility to help teach the younger women in the church. Most of the older women have already gone through many battles in life, and they know how to prevent, or at least, overcome them. I rejoice in the things I have learned throughout the years, and now I have the privilege of helping younger women learn to love their husbands and take care of their families.

The Word says women of God should live a self-controlled life. If God tells us to live self-controlled lives, that means we have the ability to do so. God never tells us to do something without giving us the power to do it. It may not be easy, but we can do it.

I have worked in the church and raised children at the same time. Under these circumstances, it's sometimes easy to lose self-control. Problems at work can make us irritable at home if we're not careful. It is easy to take out our frustrations on those people we have the most access to—our husbands and children. Instead, we should strive for self-control. If you feel your temper rising, you need to resist that temptation. Don't "blow your top."

Women are also instructed to be homemakers. What is a homemaker? It is one who manages the home and the children. Wives are called to help their husbands take care of the children and run the affairs of the house. They are to live under the authority of their husbands and be responsible to them. Remember those wonderful verses in Proverbs thirty-one?

This woman's husband loves and respects her. He has confidence in her. She takes care of herself so her husband will always be pleased with her appearance and proud of the way she looks in public as they grow old together. She is particular about her home. She wants everything to be as good as it can be. She loves to help the poor. This is a woman who knows who she is. She knows from the Word of God that she is worth something. She wants her family to be saved and covered by the blood of Jesus. She wants them to know who they are in Christ so they can accomplish all God wrote in their books of life. Through all of this, her husband and children feel blessed to have her as their wife and mother.

My husband wrote a book titled, *Things Better than Money.* One of the things John listed as being better than money was a good wife. If you're not sure you believe that, ask the man who has a bad wife.

The Position of Godly Children

Finally, as we look at God's order for families, we see how He planned for children to fit into the family unit. He expects them to live under the authority of both parents. I have counseled families where everyone's life was literally ruled by the children. God did not intend for children to dominate their parents. When it happens, life in that household is headed for disaster.

Most of the time, the wife is the one who stays home and cares for the children. Because women spend so much time with their children, it's sometimes easier for them to become lax with discipline. But consistency is vital. If children misbehave, even though they were corrected moments before, they need to be disciplined again. I can't count the number of times I have heard a mother say, "If you do that again, I am going to spank you. All right, I told you I am going to spank you. Next time, I am *really* going to spank you. I mean it!" For some mothers, it is always *next time*. Is it any wonder that soon the children begin to ignore everything she says?

When we speak to our children, they must *know* we mean what we say. If we say we are going to ground them, we'd better follow through. If we say we're going to spank them, we'd better do it. When we fail to do what we say, we train our children to disregard our words! It is important when we're parenting God's way that we be men and women of our word.

I remember an incident with David, our youngest son. We were in a mall parking lot, and he was driving. Several of my grandchildren were in the car. David was going through a phase where he just loved to shock me. As we drove around, looking for a parking space close to the store, he took a book of matches out, lit the entire pack, and put them in his mouth.

I know he expected me to get excited—to freak out, actually. But I just looked at him. "Well," I asked, "did that taste good?" He did not get the desired response. I wasn't shocked, and I did not lose my composure in front of my grandchildren. Remember, we do not have to overreact, regardless of what our children do. We don't have to take their bait every time. Raising children can be challenging, but it doesn't have to be a roller coaster of emotions.

God wants our families to be a source of love and encouragement to us. A solid Christian home—a home where we really determine to follow God's blueprint—takes a lot of hard work. It takes stewardship. We won't have that kind of home by just wanting it and asking God for it. We must make Jesus the Lord of our families. Then we need to commit to do what His Word commands. After that, God will be free to move mightily in our lives.

How does all this relate to keeping the honey in the honeymoon? Proper order is the heart of that commitment, really. I've found that it takes sharp eyes and discernment to steward a marriage, to make sure the honey that sweetens that union is not being lost to the enemy. Selfless, loving husbands and wives, people committed to the vows they have made, to the children their love has produced, and the promises they made in their youth, will long for the perfect order of a godly marriage. They will seek to please each other in every way, to rise to the level that God instructed, and to lay down their lives for the one they married.

The beautiful thing, the thing that only a loving and incredible God could devise, is that by blessing your spouse, you get blessed in return. And then you experience a joy and fulfillment that reward you beyond your wildest dreams.

"Knowing that whatsoever good thing any man doeth, the same shall he receive of the Lord..." Ephesians 6:8, KJV.

Part II

How Do I Get There from Here?

Chapter 5

Confronting Events from Our Pasts

A lot of times when I am in counseling situations, I encounter people who are truly bewildered by their own behavior—by the way they react to their spouses or to their children. They want to be different; they recognize their own shortcomings, but no amount of effort brings change. How can this be? The Apostle Paul talked about this phenomenon; he even struggled with it himself. In Romans 7:19-20, Paul says, *"For what I do is not the good I want to do; no, the evil I do not want to do—this I keep on doing. Now if I do what I do not want to do, it is no longer I who do it, but it is sin living in me that does it"* NIV.

Children learn to do the same things they see their parents do. And once they're all grown up, if they haven't dealt with those behaviors, even if they know better and want to change, they will keep right on doing those things they learned as a child! Many churches refer to those inherited or learned behaviors as generational tendencies or *ancestral spirits*. We also say people are *bent* a certain way, or they behave exactly like their mothers or their fathers.

These family tendencies can take a big toll on marriage relationships. What kind of tendencies are we talking about? Fear of communication, fear of rejection, and fear of intimacy, just to name a few. Many homes in the 40s, 50s, and even the early 60s were quite conservative and struggled with a lack of displayed affection. I have talked to many adults who were seldom hugged and kissed as children. As a result, they have a hard time receiving affection today. Many of them manage to kiss and hug their children, but they struggle with feelings of discomfort when touched by their spouses. That is so sad.

I know when John and I hear something stirring or motivational when we're in a church service or a conference, we automatically look at each other; we smile or nod. Often we hold hands. We are sharing that moment, knowing that we're experiencing the same reaction or that it has triggered a memory within us. I love the feel of his hand on my back when we walk through a room. I cherish the looks he gives me as dearly as I cherish his touch. So when I hear about husbands or wives who draw away from any kind of physical contact, I know how much they are missing. But there is hope. There is a way to go back, to learn to appreciate and even long for a touch from your spouse.

Communication is another area where people struggle. Part of the reason is that communication constantly evolves in our society. For example, today we understand that it is best to be straightforward and honest with children. One reason for that stems from the excessive amount of child sexual abuse that has come to light in recent years. We had to learn to tell children *what* they should be afraid of—to tell them that they had a right to protect their own bodies.

One woman I know grew up in a home where the father always made light of rape reports. He told his daughters, "A woman can run a lot faster with her skirt up than a man can with his pants down." To him it was a joke. He grew up in the 20s, when the world was, perhaps, a little less threatening. But this woman and her sisters lived near a man who preyed on little girls. He abused all of them over an extended period of time. Why? Because each of those little girls believed she was at fault—she should have run! None of them ever blamed the man or reported him because their father, by the words he taught them, had brought condemnation to their hearts.

Communication is vital. Those parents who grew up without learning to communicate, without the skill to speak easily to their children, need to learn how to overcome that reluctance to share their feelings and find victory.

Many of today's parents grew up in homes where children were "seen and not heard." While divorce rates were lower a few decades ago, there was no guarantee that the marriage relationships were better. Often fathers did not participate in the care and training of their children. They were present in body but absent in spirit. Control was a big issue. Frequently children heard: *Don't ask questions! Do what you're told. Because I said so. Just because.*

It is true that parents still say things like that occasionally. I can remember saying those things at times when I had a lot on my mind or times when I hadn't stopped to give one of my children my complete attention.

But in a lot of ways, communication between parents and children has improved. Most of us have learned that children are people. They deserve reasons and explanations. In fact, children respond very well to rules when they understand the *reason* for the rule.

Today we have to deal with the ancestral spirits and family tendencies that came out of those over-controlled homes of he past: Shyness. Fear. The inability to speak up, state an opinion, or make a decision. Shyness plagues some people all their lives. God may have gifted them to preach or teach or lead people at work. But they are so inhibited, so programmed to do what they are told and never make waves or assert themselves, that they turn away from God's call on their lives.

People who have been overly controlled can suffer from fear. If they grew up having a ten p.m. curfew, were never allowed to go to parties or events with their friends, were never given the opportunity to discipline themselves and make their own decisions, they may have a tendency to fear everything about the world.

They can be fearful in traffic, obsessive about door locks, about going to malls, theaters and restaurants. In extreme cases, these people can refuse to leave their homes at all. The damage done by over-controlling and over-protective parents can be extreme. By not allowing their children to grow up naturally, to explore and learn to trust the world around them, they planted seeds of anxiety, distrust and insecurity. But praise God! He offers hope, healing and health in all these situations.

Ancestral spirits can take on many forms. There are spirits of lying, infidelity, stealing, laziness, yelling and screaming, impatience and addiction. There are spirits of hiding and spirits of performance. How many remember the prevailing attitude that always asked, "What will people think?" In many homes, it didn't matter what was *real* as long as the family could project a respectable image.

In spite of today's headlines regarding the sexual exploitation of children, it is clear this problem is not a new one. In the past, such abuse was simply hidden, swept under the carpets, and it often wore a nice respectable mask. Just like the father who inadvertently taught his daughters that rape was a woman's fault, other forms of sexual abuse against children were frequently ignored or blamed on the child. Those kinds of problems do not go away just because the child grows up. Ask any pastor or counselor who spends hours trying to find the reasons for people's fears, anger, and the oppressive sense of hopelessness that so often surrounds them.

That tendency to ask, *"What will people think?"* is very destructive. It annihilates trust. And when children can't trust their parents, they suffer in many ways. When parents scream, curse and yell at their children behind closed doors, and then act very sweet in public or at church, the children view the parents as hypocrites. Often those parents add to the problem by being critical and judgmental when they see other parents scream or lose control.

Criticism, Judgment and Intolerance

Many experts agree that we are usually the most critical of flaws in others that we also see in *ourselves*. That information should bring revelation. If you find yourself getting angry and critical of certain behaviors all the time, look deep into your own heart. Is this a behavior or characteristic you dislike in yourself? Are you in denial about it? How damaging it must be when children have to listen to their parents condemn others for something they do themselves all the time at home.

Also, once a child views their mother or father as a hypocrite, the child begins to doubt the wisdom of everything that parent says. If they lie about one thing, why should the child trust them about anything else? Parents who are hypocritical about fairly insignificant issues, such as someone else's housekeeping or promptness, might jeopardize their child's respect in important issues like sexual behavior, morality, or honesty.

The tendency toward secrecy marred many of today's adults, even though it was an accepted practice in society a few years ago. People hid things like a spouse who drank too much, 'early' babies, mental illness, cheating husbands, grandparents who had lost touch with reality (I remember when people would say old folks had gone mad or lost their mind), slow learners and children with birth defects. We all know children like to talk about and share the things going on in their lives. So in households where something was hidden, the parents had to tell their children to lie. They had to come right out and train the children to tell an untruth at school, at church, or when talking with their friends.

What did that teach? It taught people that lying was all right, even necessary. Thousands of people struggle to be truthful today because they were taught as children that certain lies were okay. And like all ancestral spirits that plague families, the behavior perpetuates itself. When the grown child has children, he or she carefully teaches those children to hide the truth, cover up deficiencies, and worry about what people will think.

That continuation from one generation to the next passes the same ancestral spirit right down the family line. And remember, the Word says, *"For we wrestle not against flesh and blood, but against principalities, against powers, against the rulers of the darkness of this world, against spiritual wickedness in high places"* Ephesians 6:12, KJV.

These generational tendencies are caused by *spirits*. They are forces that want to keep families enslaved, downtrodden and always coming short of their potential. Another scripture tells us, *"The LORD is slow to anger, abounding in love and forgiving sin and rebellion. Yet he does not leave the guilty unpunished; he punishes the children for the sin of the fathers to the third and fourth generation"* Numbers 14:18, NIV.

That is one of those scriptures that is often misunderstood. It isn't that God wants to punish us. He just understood the cause of many family traits from the beginning. He knows that children learn what they live. So, when parents make bad choices, when they practice evil or dysfunctional behavior in front of their children, that behavior, or spirit, will attach itself to the family. It will hold on tenaciously until someone in that lineage falls down at the foot of the cross and asks God for deliverance.

Sounds simple, right? Let me tell you, it's hard. It's hard to even see or feel the spirits that have tormented us since we were young. And even after we receive revelation, even after we accept the fact that ancestral spirits have plagued us from birth, we have to get the courage to let God bring healing.

Spirits of addiction are some of the hardest to abandon. They feel good—for a season. Alcohol numbs the pain of daily living. Cigarettes give a little rush and a sense of comfort.

Everyone on the planet knows by now that smoking is dangerous to health. But the momentary comfort, the immediate gratification of smoking a cigarette, has more power than the fear of what will eventually happen. Scientists now say that the children of alcoholics have a greater risk of becoming alcoholics. And we know that the children of smokers are more likely to smoke. The secular world may not call this a manifestation of ancestral spirits. But whatever they call it, it is true that addictions, tendencies and bad habits follow family lines.

It is also true that God offers a solution that works and a hope that can produce freedom. And not just for spirits of addiction. God can help defeat all those spirits that have enslaved families for generations.

In Matthew 12:43-45, Jesus said, *"When an evil spirit comes out of a man, it goes through arid places seeking rest and does not find it. Then it says, 'I will return to the house I left.' When it arrives, it finds the house unoccupied, swept clean and put in order. Then it goes and takes with it seven other spirits more wicked than itself, and they go in and live there. And the final condition of that man is worse than the first"* NIV.

How Family Tendencies Affect Our Lives

Ancestral spirits are serious business. Entertaining a lie can open the door to cheating, stealing, and corruption. It can start innocently enough as a little white lie, a lie told to spare another's feelings. (Hint: That's where the old adage, "If you can't think of something nice to say, say *nothing at all,*" will come in handy.)

But lies are as fertile as mice. One leads to another. That one lie generates the need for still another one. Soon people begin to lie out of habit. Their consciences are seared. They no longer see that telling the truth is important. The strange thing is that they never really get away with it. Once people catch them in one lie, they expect everything else they say to be false.

I understand this can be a touchy subject. Is it a lie when we say we will be somewhere at noon and we don't arrive until twelve-fifteen? Certainly traffic accidents, car trouble or unavoidable delays can make this happen to anyone once in a while. But when we oversleep, and we blame it on car trouble, once the truth comes out, will we ever be trusted again? Maybe not. At least until we build a better track record. It is important to tell the truth. Even on those occasions when it isn't easy.

It may not seem important to unveil every ancestral spirit, but it is. Many people are guilty of thinking of sins in degrees. For instance, if a little white lie is a one and murder is a ten—what is shoplifting? To God, I think they are all tens. The Word says, *"Anyone, then, who knows the good he ought to do and doesn't do it, sins"* James 4:17, NIV.

Many church people would never think of running a scam on elderly people. That is cheating! But they may habitually tell little white lies on the telephone. Sometimes they even tell big lies to creditors or to get out of an obligation. Are the children watching? What have they just learned? This should make us all examine ourselves.

Some people play with the numbers on their income tax returns. It is all right to diligently seek out every legitimate deduction. But is it all right to hide income that isn't traceable? Is that cheating? It seems the enemy likes to draw us close to breaking one of the Ten Commandments, knowing once we play along the borders, we may be tempted to step across the line.

What about these other tendencies that dwell in so many homes: impatience, anger, cursing, yelling, and even physical violence? Those things cause such deep wounds in children. They hurt their feelings; they attack their self-image; and ultimately, they cause the child to grow up and repeat the behavior.

I've noticed very few parents like to admit they are screamers. Often it comes out when the child tells someone or exhibits screaming behavior of their own. Physical violence is different. It leaves marks. And, once seen, it *must* be reported. People have told me they feel helpless when it comes to their anger issues, that they have tried everything to gain self-control. Have they tried putting their anger at the foot of the cross? God can and will heal people who truly repent. But He cannot heal people who hide behind their family tendencies and defend and protect their behavior, blaming it on others or saying it doesn't exist.

Spirits of lying, cheating, stealing, infidelity, untrustworthiness, chronic tardiness, unreliability, and exaggeration are closely connected. One often leads to another. If a child grows up with spirits of lying, hiding and performance, he might just go ahead and embrace cheating, stealing, and untrustworthiness as an adult.

Any of these family tendencies can take a staggering toll on a marriage once an unsuspecting husband or wife becomes aware of it.

Spirits of Depression

Depression can also be a family tendency. The devil likes to make people (particularly women who stay home all day) think they are overwhelmed, that they can't handle all they are supposed to do. Instead of doing a few things, sometimes they do nothing. The house gets dirty. The children don't look as clean and neat as they should.

A woman's depression will cause a lot of honey to drip out of the honeymoon. And it can drive a husband away. There are many reasons she could find herself under that level of attack. Maybe she watches too much television. Think about the kinds of spirits you might be inviting into your home if the television set is constantly tuned to soap operas or talk shows. You watch people yell and scream and accuse each other relentlessly on those programs, and they parade every possible kind of perversion across the screen. Are those the topics and ideas you want to invite into your living room?

Maybe the depressed woman feels guilty. Maybe her husband would like her to get a job outside the home to help the family financially. Maybe he is overly critical or unkind. Depression and poor self-image in women often comes from little or poor relationships with men. If she didn't learn to love herself and see her own value in her father's eyes, she may have gone through a period of promiscuity or desperately seeking a man's love and approval. Such a woman could feel very guilty. She would be willing to marry anyone who would have her. Unfortunately, many selfish and insensitive men are masters at spotting such vulnerable women. Once they are married, no matter how hard she tries to please that kind of man, it will never be enough. He will easily control her just by attacking her looks, her abilities, or her self-worth.

This is not the way God planned her life and her marriage to be. He can heal depression but she will have to ask Him.

Ancestral Spirits Can Sabotage A Marriage

The enemy loves to use ancestral spirits to tear families down, generation after generation. He doesn't care whether he uses control, selfishness, cheating, lying, nagging, screaming, or any other negative behavior, if he can get husbands and wives to stubbornly follow the patterns they learned as children, he can shoot holes into their relationship.

God can heal marriages where a lack of stewardship and compassion have brought both husband and wife to the point that neither one of them wants to make the first move toward reconciliation. Sometimes I wonder how couples survive in homes like that, how they manage to avoid discussing the dirty house, or the fact that the husband does nothing after he gets home except sit down in front of a television set and stay there until he goes to bed.

I would recommend that couples caught in traps like these break every habit and pattern they have allowed to take over their lives. They need to go to church. They need to make friends with couples who are living more ordered and successful lives. They need to spend time together and rediscover those things they once found beautiful and exciting about each other.

Such a marriage needs a *lot* of prayer. Christians who know those kinds of couples, need to stand in the gap for them, interceding often. This is a situation where almost every ounce of honey has already trickled away. We all need to do a honey check on our marriages once in a while. Are there still plenty of sweet words? The Bible says, *"Pleasant words are a honeycomb, sweet to the soul and healing to the bones"* Proverbs 16:24, NIV. When the pleasant words begin to disappear, it is a sure sign the honey is escaping somewhere.

There is a spirit of laziness, and I think it's attached to the spirit of selfishness. Sometimes couples don't want to do the jobs and chores that are their responsibility. Maybe they want to watch TV or go out with their friends. Maybe they just want to sleep late or go to the mall or play golf. Without help from the Holy Ghost, that kind of laziness can control a person for his or her entire life.

There are two other generational tendencies that I want to mention before I end this chapter. Both of them can cause major dysfunction in a person's life and could require professional help. The first one is hypochondria. That is a condition where people suffer from one illness after another. They use their symptoms and illnesses as a reason to stay indoors, or to keep from working, or to hide from the tasks and activities of normal life. In many cases these illnesses are used to avoid the responsibilities of marriage.

Doctor's appointments, hospital stays, and a search for sympathy become the only important events for some of these people. Their illnesses, imagined illnesses, and self-absorbed worry take over every aspect of life. This has to be very hard for a spouse to endure, and even harder on their marriage and the home.

The other spirit that attacks some people is a love for turmoil and high drama. There are individuals who move from one crisis to the next, not feeling fully alive unless their lives are in an uproar. Their marriage is constantly in upheaval. Big fights erupt, police officers are called. The children run away. Appliances break, tires blow, they can't keep a job. Drama and disaster are daily events.

What is going on in their lives? It seems the events really do occur, but why? What makes the people in that home willing to live every moment at such an accelerated pace? It's usually an ancestral spirit, a way of life that was learned at an early age.

This chapter has been difficult to write. There have been times when I felt like every one of those spirits was sitting on my back and my shoulders, trying desperately to keep me from writing these words and exposing them. But they are exposed! They are laid bare in the light of day. Ephesians 5:14 says, "*...for it is light that makes everything visible. This is why it is said: 'Wake up, O sleeper, rise from the dead, and Christ will shine on you'*" NIV.

The first step to overcoming and defeating those old family traits in our lives is simply to expose them to Christ's light. We need to look at them and recognize they don't really have much power since Jesus defeated them (Colossians 2:15). And then we need to lay them before the Lord and let the blood of Jesus' love and redemption wash them away.

We do not have to lie. We do not have to be depressed. We do not have to hide our shortcomings, or live in a 'performance' mode all the time. When we defeat the spirits that conspire to destroy our marriages, we seal up those wounds in our relationships where the honey can be lost.

God loves us. He adores us in spite of the things we have suffered, the tendencies that have attached themselves to us, or the bad things we may have done in our lives. God is waiting to heal us, to embrace us with His anointing, His approval and His unfailing grace.

Chapter 6

Money, Money, Money

Money, children and sex are listed most frequently as the reasons married couples argue. In this chapter, we will focus on money. How can something that has the potential to bring so much pleasure and freedom also be the cause of so much strife? It's because financial matters are one of the enemy's favorite areas of attack. And from what I hear in counseling sessions, it doesn't matter how much money a family has—they still can get into conflict over it.

Arguments over money can be bitter. They cause deep wounds that allow the honey to flood out of the honeymoon in great waves. Things are often said by both husband and wife, that can be hard to forget, let alone forgive.

Too much money is usually not quite as disruptive as too little, but it can still bring an opportunity for disagreement. Unless a husband and wife lay down the ground rules about money early on, they can expect trouble. What are those ground rules? Can they really prevent the conflicts that plague so many marriages?

First, let's talk about quarrels over money, how they start, and why they are so destructive to marital harmony. I have met with couples that struggled so often over finances that it was almost the only thing they ever discussed. Once money issues get a toehold in a marriage, once the battle lines are drawn and both partners hunker down in their foxholes, everything else becomes secondary.

One couple I counseled was having trouble with rebellious and angry children. They had two, both preteens. Neither of the children would speak to the father—not when he came home from work, not at the dinner table and not even when he addressed them directly. He had reached a point where he was ready to move out.

It turned out the wife was very unhappy with the amount of money he was earning. She didn't work outside the home. The husband's company had downsized, and he had taken a pay cut, believing things would improve eventually and grateful he hadn't been laid off.

But there are always a lot of expenses required in raising children, including clothing, shoes, school supplies, and funds for extra curricular activities. Every time these children approached their mother for money, she told them the family was broke. She worded it in such a way that the children blamed their father and grew more and more angry with him. The wife had compounded the problem by not standing behind her husband. She had failed to support him or explain that it was probably a temporary situation. Because of her response, the children lost respect for their father, and a loss of respect is a terrible thing.

As we worked with this couple, it became obvious the wife was angry, and she had punished her husband by turning the children against him. She was fortunate. He forgave her. Many husbands would not have been that gracious with the level of betrayal she displayed. We thank God for the honey being restored in that home.

Money generates high levels of emotion. It causes people to do things they might not normally do. Money can cause fear. I have counseled a number of "hoarders," people so frightened by the idea they might run out of money that they hide it, or steal it out of household funds, and lie about their behavior. Any time a husband or wife starts to lie, trouble is coming in that home.

I believe hoarders are frequently women, but there is another behavior, and it is often attributed to men. Those are the people who spend wildly (often on gambling debts or sports-related expenses), and then go to incredible lengths to hide the evidence. These individuals always want to answer the telephone and bring in the mail. I met with one woman whose husband insisted he handle the bills. He constantly assured her that their financial status was fine. One day her son brought her an enormous pile of unpaid bills that the husband had been hiding under the child's mattress. How long did this man think he could possibly cover a problem of such magnitude?

It turned out he was involved in gambling. He would say he was going on a business trip, but he would actually travel to Las Vegas or Reno. He ran up expenses on the company credit cards. He tapped out every financial resource his family had. Eventually that marriage failed because of the shocking disregard the husband showed for the welfare of his family, and because his wife was unable to forgive him.

You can see from these examples how powerfully money affects emotions. Are these cases extreme? Perhaps. Are they rare? No. Christians can get into just as much trouble as people in the secular world if they start making bad choices. Remember, God said, *"...I have set before you life and death, blessings and curses. Now choose life, so that you and your children may live"* Deuteronomy 30:19, NIV.

Sometimes Christians get so involved in Christian television, seminars, and conferences that they begin giving money without even asking God where He desires them to make their offerings. Many times I've seen good families who have been blessed by God just give their blessings away. God wants us to enjoy some of the bounty He gives us (for ourselves, our children, and our home). You should always be in agreement with your spouse about the ministries and missions you will support.

We have looked at a calculating wife who wanted to punish her husband through the children, and we have seen a husband lured into gambling and other sins who was willing to jeopardize his family's security and happiness. Quarreling, punishment, loss of respect, and manipulation are just a few of the negative results that occur when the love of money takes over in a home.

Of course, money problems don't affect all marriages this severely. But even when the circumstances are not so dramatic, damage can be extensive. Imagine a couple that argues about money in front of the children, or in front of other relatives and friends. They snipe at each other and insult each other so often that they no longer realize their remarks are shooting poison arrows right into the heart of their marriage, causing precious honey to drip out every time an arrow penetrates.

Another problem I've noticed is when a couple makes the decision to keep their money in separate accounts. They treat their finances like a business. Each of them maintains control over his or her own income. Maybe the wife is afraid of losing her independence. Maybe the husband is fearful that his new wife will be careless with money, so he decides not to let her have access to his checkbook. This can be a very big danger sign. If there were such things as marriage referees, flags would be thrown all over the field.

Instead of setting up separate checking accounts, I believe these couples should discuss their fears, openly voice their expectations, and reach a compromise that signifies their love and trust for each other. Why? Because refusing to trust each other with their income shows a lack of agreement from the beginning. It says, "*We're not really in this thing with all our hearts*." It takes trust to let a new wife sign on a checking account. It takes trust for a new wife, one who has always worked and paid her own way, to deposit her money into an account where someone else can spend it.

If they refuse to trust each other, they will soon be in as much trouble as the first two couples. Little by little, day after day, couples such as these let the honey seep out of their honeymoon. In fact, most of them are so war-torn by the time I see them that they can't remember when they were in love or what it felt like to desire to spend time with each other.

Is there a cure? Is there hope? Can respect and love be reborn from the ashes of a burned-out marriage? Yes. But *everything* has to change. Couples have to stop, regroup, lay down their pride and their egos, and they have to want to put their family back together.

There used to be a medical practice called "patterning." They used it for autistic children or when children were not developing correctly or at a pace with their peers. It was a process where they went all the way back to the moment the child was learning to crawl, and they reproduced the steps of crawling one by one, in hopes the child would then progress at the normal rate.

That's what these broken marriages need. They need to go back to the moment when the husband and wife were first learning to set financial priorities, when they were deciding what their family would value, where they would spend, when they would spend, what they would require and what they would be willing to do without.

As we go over these steps, as we look at the things a couple has to do to salvage their financial relationship, understand that these are the same steps a newly married couple would go through. I hope and pray your family will get it right the first time, without going through the fires of financial tribulation that so many others endure.

Financial Agreement

If there is a single word that could set a couple on the right path when it comes to money, it would have to be *agreement*. You have to talk. You need to list the things you value, the financial goals you would like to reach in your marriage, and the ideas and opinions you have about money. Were your parents good with money? Did they have shared goals? Was money used as a weapon or a power tool in either of your homes as children?

It is absolutely imperative that you talk about the way you feel about tithing, offerings, and charity. Is Jesus going to be the head of your home? If so, you will have to follow the biblical teachings about marriage, parenting, and finances.

How do you feel about loans? About paying interest? Are you willing to wait for some things in order to pay cash or to pay the least amount of interest possible? What kinds of expenses do you consider most important when it comes to your children? Is education a priority? Will you start savings accounts as soon as the children are born?

It amazes me how people will not start driving across the country to go to Disneyland without getting their hands on an atlas and a few good maps. But these same people will start maneuvering through the intricacies of family life without even bothering to discuss their values and the things they hope to achieve.

Let's assume our couple determines that Jesus is indeed Lord over their home, and they both want to give tithes and offerings on a regular basis. Good choice! Now God can really go to work on blessing them.

Biblical Economics

I want to talk for just a moment about what the Bible has to say about tithes and offerings. The best-known scripture is in the Old Testament. *"Will a man rob God? Yet you rob me. But you ask, 'How do we rob you?' In tithes and offerings. You are under a curse—the whole nation of you—because you are robbing me. Bring the whole tithe into the storehouse, that there may be food in my house. Test me in this," says the LORD Almighty, "and see if I will not throw open the floodgates of heaven and pour out so much blessing that you will not have room enough for it. I will prevent pests from devouring your crops, and the vines in your fields will not cast their fruit," says the LORD Almighty. "Then all the nations will call you blessed, for yours will be a delightful land," says the LORD Almighty"* Malachi 3:8-12, NIV.

A tithe is ten percent. God blesses us so richly and abundantly, and He expects us to return ten percent of that income to Him. Why? He says so there will be food in His storehouse. The church is His storehouse. And the church is responsible for gathering God's money to pay expenses and distribute to the poor both locally and around the world.

Money is not only an emotional topic in many homes, it is an emotional topic in churches as well. People who do not understand how godly finances work are constantly defensive about pastors asking for money. I know in my church I talk about money frequently because I want people to understand I am trying to get money *to* them, not *from* them.

My husband, John, is one of the foremost teachers on the subject of biblical economics. Certainly he was one of the first to have the courage to teach people that God wants them to prosper. Years ago, there was a widely held philosophy that Christians needed to be poor. And pastors needed to be poorer still! Why would people have believed that? The Bible is full of Scriptures about barns overflowing, olive trees and grapevines heavy with fruit, and other prosperity promises. And these Scriptures aren't simply referring to prosperity in the hereafter, but rather right now, in this lifetime.

But people misunderstood the Word. They thought Jesus was poor, so His followers should be poor as well. We now know that Jesus was not poor! In His time, He was quite well to do. I don't want to get into that teaching here, but a careful study of the gospels will prove that Jesus wanted for nothing. He was not a beggar. He always paid His own way.

So we see in Malachi that God will throw open the floodgates of heaven over us when we tithe. But He didn't say people were robbing Him with just their tithes (their ten percent). He said they were robbing Him in tithes *and* offerings. Now when we give our tithes, God opens the windows of heaven. What does He pour out? A return on our offerings! *"Others, like seed sown on good soil, hear the word, accept it, and produce a crop—thirty, sixty or even a hundred times what was sown"* Mark 4:20, NIV.

That Scripture is talking about offerings. When we sow (plant seed) into the Kingdom of God, He is able to pour out through those open windows in heaven an amount thirty, sixty, even a hundred times the amount we sowed.

This may be difficult to understand if you've never heard it before. Some people are fearful that if they tithe, they will not have enough left to get by. But ask a giver. Many church people have discovered this great truth about God's promises in the Book of Malachi. He says, *"Test me in this."* And it works.

Taking Your Financial Temperature

Once a couple has agreed to start over, to learn each other's values, opinions and priorities about money, once they have agreed to make Jesus Lord over their home and to give tithes and offerings, they need to sit down and get into *agreement* about their goals and how they are going to reach them.

They also need to make a budget and stick to it. How much money comes into the home? This is so important. Write it down. What are the monthly expenses? Write them down. It is impossible for husbands and wives to be good stewards over their money if they don't even know what their income and their outgo are.

Once they make their budget, many couples realize why they are in trouble. They are living way above their means. They have to make decisions and come up with a strategy to correct the problem. Should the wife go to work? If she is already working, where can they cut expenses? Do they have any prospects to increase their income? Should they reduce their monthly expenses by lowering their lifestyle? I have seen couples that were willing to sell a car or their home, rethink a wife's job and daycare costs, and to absolutely stop using credit cards once they took a good honest look at their financial situation.

This assessment is mandatory. Once they realize how far they have to go, they can make a plan for getting there. In my church, the ultimate goal of our couples is to be debt free. In fact, we had a speaker one time that said, "If people can't be debt free in this church, they might as well give up!" It was funny, but it was also true. My husband, John, is relentless in his teaching that God wants to bless us, that He wants to see us prosper, and that we can't be blessings to others if we're worried about making our own house payment.

Did you know you're supposed to be a blessing to others? That's right. If you intend to fulfill the Great Commission, the last command that Jesus gave us before He ascended into heaven, you *have* to bless others. *"Therefore go and make disciples of all nations, baptizing them in the name of the Father and of the Son and of the Holy Spirit, and teaching them to obey everything I have commanded you. And surely I am with you always, to the very end of the age"* Matthew 28:19-20, NIV.

Jesus would not have told us to travel to the ends of the earth, teaching His message and baptizing people if He didn't intend for us to be able to pay for those trips, as well as fund the television and radio stations that broadcast the message. Airfare is expensive. Airtime is expensive. Books cost a lot to produce. Teaching everything Jesus taught requires a lot of television programs, overnight stays—days or even weeks in every location. Hotels cost a lot of money, and so does food.

So in order to bless others, we must have enough money to give generously into the Kingdom of God. We have a young couple in our church that bought a home nine years ago, and they have managed to pay off that house completely. That's right. They are debt free and they have a nice home. The young husband caught the vision first. He explained his plan to his wife, and they got into agreement about accomplishing their goal. They budgeted everything. He told our people one night at church that he even budgets toothpaste. But that may be what it takes.

A vision does not usually come to fruition overnight. It is line upon line, precept upon precept, a little here and a little there. This couple is now free to go anywhere and do anything God asks them to do. Recently they were blessed with a gift of $500, and they immediately gave it away to others. That's how God's plan works. He can bless people who understand the principle of blessing others.

Once you have set your budget and your goals, what next? You must persevere. When temptations come against you—let's say there's a big sale on something you have determined to purchase in another year—you *must* stick to your budget. The enemy is not going to be happy when you begin to live your life God's way. The devil thought he had you in his pocket, signed, sealed and delivered, but you got away. Praise God!

So stick to your budget. Don't turn aside. What rewards will you reap? More than you can imagine or count. First, since you are working for a common goal, side by side, you and your spouse will grow closer. You will maintain, or even rediscover the love that first brought you together. By tithing and giving offerings, you will be able to enjoy the grace and blessings of the Lord. Many couples say the ninety percent they keep after they start tithing goes much further than one hundred percent did before.

How can that be? It's more practical than mystical. God will lead you to incredible bargains. Your appliances, cars and clothing will literally last longer.

A man in our church had to spend a season working in another city, and the extra mileage was beginning to wear on his car. One evening he was making the drive back to Fort Worth when he began to experience big problems with his transmission. He started to pray as the car lurched down the street, "I'm a tither, Lord. I live under an open heaven. This ought not to be." Miraculously, within a few blocks the car started to run smoothly again. When he had it checked by his mechanic the following day, there was no evidence of the problem.

Because John and I speak at churches all over the world, we hear stories like this all the time. Tithing works. Committing marriages and families to God works. The rewards are great. *"Now to Him who is able to do exceedingly abundantly above all that we ask or think, according to the power that works in us, to Him be glory...."* Ephesians 3:20-21, NKJV.

Imagine a marriage free of discord over money. Imagine a home where there is enough money to meet the monthly expenses, where unexpected repairs can be covered, and where the cost of a child's education is not a burden. Imagine seeing a person who has a great need, and being free to meet that need on the spot. That is God's plan for you.

He does not want us to suffer the humiliation of late payments and the abuse that people who are in deep debt must often endure. And once we get to that wonderful place of being debt free, let me encourage one other step.

Be generous. Be merciful. Remember the servant in the Bible who was forgiven the great debt? Let's look at what Jesus had to say about that. "*...The kingdom of heaven is like a king who wanted to settle accounts with his servants. As he began the settlement, a man who owed him ten thousand talents was brought to him. Since he was not able to pay, the master ordered that he and his wife and his children and all that he had be sold to repay the debt. The servant fell on his knees before him. 'Be patient with me,' he begged, 'and I will pay back everything.' The servant's master took pity on him, canceled the debt and let him go. But when that servant went out, he found one of his fellow servants who owed him a hundred denarii. He grabbed him and began to choke him. 'Pay back what you owe me!' he demanded. His fellow servant fell to his knees and begged him, 'Be patient with me, and I will pay you back.' But he refused. Instead, he went off and had the man thrown into prison until he could pay the debt. When the other servants saw what had happened, they were greatly distressed and went and told their master everything that had happened. Then the master called the servant in. 'You wicked servant,' he said, 'I canceled all that debt of yours because you begged me to. Shouldn't you have had mercy on your fellow servant just as I had on you?' In anger his master turned him over to the jailers to be tortured, until he should pay back all he owed. This is how my heavenly Father will treat each of you unless you forgive your brother from your heart*" Matthew 18:23-35, NIV.

Money has tremendous power. Not on its own, of course, but because the world gives it that power. It can cause heartache, suffering, manipulation, crime, and the loss of human dignity and honor, or it can bring healing, love, relief, nourishment, and satisfaction. Money is no greater, and it is no less important than we think it is.

How we feel about money, how we let it affect us, can make a huge difference in the level of peace and joy we find in our marriages. God wants us to have money. He just doesn't want money to have us.

Chapter 7

Children, a Built-in Tower of Power

I enjoy watching young couples as they anticipate the arrival of their first baby. They have such great hopes, idealistic expectations, and there is a wonderful childish innocence about them. Parenting is one of the sweetest joys God has entrusted to us. But there are times, and plenty of them, when the joys of parenthood can turn ugly.

Children will try to get away with anything they can. They will try to gain a position of power, aiming their cute little smiles and their adorable ways straight at the heart of their parents' marriage—controlling the meals, the family outings, the television set, the free time, and the mood that prevails in the home.

As I watch expectant parents, I am concerned that they may not have a realistic idea of the task before them. There is a big difference between the concept of parenthood while a couple is expecting, and the reality of parenthood once the child is born.

The birth of a child is the beginning of a long parenting journey. It will have ups and downs. Parents will learn from their children, they will learn from others, and they will learn from their mistakes. Parenting can be one of the most rewarding times in a couple's lives, or it can mark the beginning of a nightmare. It is pointless to frighten expectant parents with the negative things that can happen. Everyone's experience is different.

I remember making plans for my own children long before they were born. I only wanted two, so I would always be able to keep their clothes washed and ironed and their little white high-top shoes polished. Back then it was thought that the high-top shoes strengthened their ankles. Well, I had my plans, but God's plans were different.

John and I had four children in four and a half years. Would you say that was an excellent example of planned parenthood? Ha!

Later, our four children began to pray for a baby brother. Every Wednesday night at church when John asked the people if they had any prayer requests, there would be our son, Buc's, little hand waving in the air. John *knew* what the prayer request would be, but he couldn't ignore him. As soon as his father called on him, Buc would say, "Pray we get a baby brother."

Prayer works! God put it in our hearts to have another baby, and we praise Him. That little brother's name is David, and the anointing to get the body out of debt lives in him and his wife, Michelle.

When it came to raising children, I never wanted to make the mistakes I felt my parents had made. And I *didn't* repeat those mistakes. I made brand new ones. Lots of them. When I talk to other parents, I find they've had that same experience. Most of us love our children dearly. We want what is best for them. Our intentions are pure. But wanting to be a good parent and being one are two different things.

There are more books out there on this subject than just about any other topic. The secular world, the Christian community, the medical people, and the scientific and academic folks have all had a go at it. Who is right? Whose ideas are the ones that will best equip a couple to raise a child?

God's ideas are the best. And He knew the importance of this subject. In the King James Version of the Bible, there are 1802 references to the word children and 201 references to the word child. Was God trying to tell us something? Prepare us for a job that would be challenging, puzzling, and more difficult than any new parent could ever imagine? Yes, He was.

He knew the world would want to steal our influence with our children, that Madison Avenue would lure them with advertising, that the tobacco industry and the alcohol makers would tempt them, the entertainment industry would court them, political parties would try to mold and engineer their thinking, and every tennis shoe maker, music group, and media source in the nation would try to convert them to a specific point of view.

It's hard to imagine that the young people who listen to violent rap songs today, to hard core rock that advocates premarital sex, crime and the use of drugs, were once small innocents who loved to watch Mr. Rogers, Captain Kangaroo, or Barney. When do children change? What is the age? How can we keep a level of influence in their lives that will shelter them from dangerous and destructive choices once they get older?

I remember a time when one of my children was tempted by drugs. John and I were out of town, and she had gone to a friend's home. It wasn't a wild party, just a group of kids, but suddenly someone brought out marijuana and started to pass it around. My daughter heard a siren outside, an ambulance or a fire truck. She thought the Rapture had come, and she jumped up, ran outside, and began begging God for forgiveness. God's influence, and our influence, helped her make a correct choice.

It really helps when we take children to church when they are small. *"Train up a child in the way he should go: and when he is old, he will not depart from it"* Proverbs 22:6, NKJV. We need to explain to our children that the world wants to lure them into every form of debt, perversion, and temptation. They are commodities. That's how the world views them. They are a resource with a pocketful of money and an earning capacity that can be plundered.

But I am getting way ahead of myself. Let's go back to the cute little couple waiting for the birth of that first child. There are so many ways they can get off on the wrong foot. And in spite of that, most of us just sit back and let them plow blindly into their new roles. When John and I had our first child, there were not nearly as many books (of course there were *no* videos) to offer help and suggestions. But there were also not as many distractions aimed directly at the child. We didn't have to compete with as much television, with computer games or with the Internet.

Establishing A Child's Order in the Home

I am not a big user of computers but I certainly am aware of the lure of e-mail, chat rooms, online shopping and the thousands of entertainment choices offered on the web. There are many wonderful things online. But there are also treacherous people, dangerous ideas, perversion and physical harm waiting for the child who is poorly supervised. The same is true, of course, with cable television. These are perilous times in which to let a television set or a computer babysit a child.

And it isn't just school-age children who are at risk. When our young parents bring their baby home from the hospital, they will get all kinds of offers in the mail. There are software programs, music CD's, television videos, and countless other products aimed at the tiniest children. It is fine to get one of those classical music tapes that are meant to stimulate a child's creativity and IQ. But it is not a good idea to purchase piles of videos and plop the infant down in front of the television set.

Even tapes with a Christian message can be harmful if the child is left to interpret them alone. When children watch TV, a parent should check in with them often, offering comment, asking questions, making certain the child is not being over stimulated or getting incorrect ideas from the material.

Once again, being in agreement will be especially helpful for parents of young children. You need to get into *agreement* about every aspect of childrearing. What are your expectations and goals regarding academics, sports, music and college? What methods of discipline will you use in the home? Will correction be swift and consistent, and will it always fit the offense? Will you and your spouse stay in close communication with each other at the end of every day, defeating any attempt by your children to play you against one another?

Who will be in control? That one seems so obvious that I'm certain many young parents will find it laughable. But if you ignore it, you won't be laughing long. Babies can be tyrants. Some toddlers put dictators to shame. How? By being extremely perceptive to their parent's love and mercy.

I was a fairly strict mother, understanding biblical principles of discipline. But I have known mothers who loved their children so deeply they couldn't stand to see them punished or even scolded. Such children quickly learn to run and hide behind their mothers when there is a reason for correction. Their mothers immediately begin to plead their case and make excuses. But a mother's love should never give her an excuse to cripple and handicap her children. Protecting them from discipline will not help them. Children need to take responsibility for their actions and be held accountable when they do something wrong.

Inconsistency and over-protection also open the door for children to play one parent against the other. They might wait until the mother leaves the room, then tell their father, "Mama said it's okay" when she has not said any such thing. Or the father might say, "I don't like the idea, but go ask Mama what she thinks," and the child runs to the mother and says, "Daddy says it's okay with him if it's okay with you." Situations like that should warn you to get into agreement before making decisions, to not give any go-ahead unless you have talked to each other first.

Why do our children do such things? Well, if the parents are battling each other, they have little time or inclination to discipline the child. Once this kind of manipulation comes into play, it can knock the honey out of a honeymoon in a hurry.

What does the Bible say about this? Plenty! *"Foolishness is bound up in the heart of a child; The rod of correction will drive it far from him"* Proverbs 22:15, NKJV.

"The fear of the LORD is the beginning of knowledge, but fools despise wisdom and discipline" Proverbs 1:7, NIV.

"Even a child is known by his actions, by whether his conduct is pure and right" Proverbs 20:11, NIV.

There are many more Scriptures about discipline, children and God's expectations for our self-control. Rebellious, manipulative children are not a new phenomenon. Cain killed Abel, remember? And when that happened, I wonder if Eve pleaded his case, saying, "But you know he always felt inferior, Adam. You know Abel couldn't stop gloating and trying to push Cain's buttons."

It is discouraging to watch the news on television or to read the paper when we see that young people are committing crimes that are increasingly violent. Many are showing a callous disregard for the pain and suffering of others. And even in those extreme cases, the parents often make excuses and defend their children.

I remember a time when one of our children came home with our Ford Ranger and the top was all smashed. The story he told me about how it happened had me defending and protecting my child immediately. Twenty years later, I finally heard the truth. My child was in the wrong place, a place he was not supposed to be, and he turned the car over. Daddy wasn't home (he was never as easy to deceive as I was), and my child fooled me completely.

Supporting and defending a child may seem like a favor at the moment of crisis, but when children are not required to take responsibility for their actions, when they never have to be punished or even made to understand the severity of the things they have done, it can hamper their growth as productive and useful members of society.

I have seen parents who continued to make excuses, even when their child was accused of armed robbery or murder, and I have wondered how their situation evolved to that point. I think it happens because the same parent protected and made excuses when their child pushed another child off the slide in preschool, or when their child grabbed toys and refused to share in Kindergarten.

Such parents failed to grasp God's instruction, *"Train a child in the way he should go, and when he is old he will not turn from it"* Proverbs 22:6, NIV. They refused to understand that the momentary tears following discipline are the salve and the ointment that ensure a child's correct growth and development.

It takes courage and real love to discipline children. Parents need to understand that—to expect that. They need to take their youngsters to church, and teach them to respect Sunday school teachers and other church workers, so they will respect their school teachers and others in authority as they grow older. I am not saying that a child should be taught to be a robot, to do *anything* and *everything* an adult says. We've already talked about the inherent dangers in that.

But when a child is trained in church, when he or she attends classes and begins to learn the value of friendship and discipline, the child's parents are involved. They all go to the church together. Parents can visit the classroom any time they like. They can explain lessons a child might not understand. They can talk about respect and duty, obligation and authority. They can teach their children the value of obedience, listening, completing tasks, and acting as part of a group or a team.

Expectations from children should start early and evolve as they grow. In the beginning, there's a temptation to view the conflicts as "cute." A toddler spits carrots out or throws them around the room. That one stops being "cute" rather quickly. A baby refuses to take a nap or go to sleep, growing more and more cranky as the afternoon wears on. Or a toddler absolutely will not be potty trained. We understand that these things will eventually be accomplished. And we know it is wrong to harshly discipline a tiny child over such matters. BUT if the child wins every struggle, if he or she never naps, never eats properly, or wears diapers well into preschool, there are far worse battles ahead.

The child who wins the toddler wars will expect to win the bedtime, homework, and freedom wars that follow. I don't think it's a good idea to let ten and eleven-year-olds go to the mall with a group of their friends, but I know many parents who allow it. Why? Because they lost the right to say no a long time ago. Children will always ask to do things that are dangerous and that might cause them serious harm. They never think they will be abducted or exploited by someone at the mall. But it can happen, and it does happen.

Preteen children feel pretty grown up these days. They are sophisticated and much more aware of adult topics than I was as a child, and even as my children were. Cable television, computers, books, and regular television programming have all taken a huge portion of our children's innocence.

Children are the targets of a lot of advertising. Madison Avenue knows how to display and tantalize. Saturday morning television programming is aimed straight at our wallets. Advertisers know that kids can be very pushy and persuasive when they see something, when they think everyone else is getting it, and when they decide they just have to have it. They are masters at badgering, begging, pleading, and whining, making themselves extremely obnoxious as they lobby for the desires of their hearts.

It is at this point, once they have become the physical, emotional, and financial hostages of their children, that many permissive parents wake up. What can they do now? A lot. Even when the hard line is drawn in the sand late, it can still be drawn. Many a rebellious child has grown up and asked a parent, "Why did you let me act that way?" Children want boundaries. They want to be disciplined. They do not want to think they are just thrashing about in total rebellion when they do not yet have the skills needed for correct choices.

I've noticed that if control isn't regained by the time the child is a preteen, the battle lines get more pronounced and the stakes get higher. Soon the conflicts are over sex and drugs and alcohol, over issues like staying out all night, staying in school, disrespecting authority, and even issues of honesty, crime, and running away. Once the situation gets this bad, parents can feel helpless, often standing by and watching as their children make one bad choice after another—running with destructive friends, dropping out of school, throwing away college opportunities, and getting involved with serious social crimes. Many a promising youngster has compromised intelligence to drugs, promise to a prison term, abilities and future to the responsibilities of raising children that were born out of wedlock.

Scary stuff, huh? Not the kinds of things we want to dump on that cute little couple expecting their first baby. But sometimes I wonder when we should warn them about the things that can go wrong. Early,

I think, before they learn it the hard way. The moment they bring the baby home from the hospital they need to promise each other that they will stay in *agreement*.

New parents need to promise each other a lot of things. Society and the media have championed the decay of the family unit, opting for political correctness in its place: extended families, second families, third families, step-families, single- parent families, same-parent families—all covered with an umbrella of sentimentality that seeks to hide the pain and suffering these situations bring in real-life human terms. We have a generation of children who are angry. They are angry that their parents didn't have the discernment to wait for and to marry the person God had for them, angry that commitments were so shallow that untold thousands of marriages fail, and angry because they are not being raised by their biological fathers or mothers.

We need to make a greater effort to keep our marriage vows. Husbands and wives are not fast food. When we don't like the flavor or the service, we can't just hop on down the street to the next offering. Fathers are not hamburgers. Mothers are not tacos. Many parents have the casual attitude that it's all right to throw the other parent out the front door one day and bring a substitute in the back door the next. Because mothers often end up as the custodial parent, they exhibit this behavior more often.

Understand, I'm not letting fathers off the hook. Many times they don't want custody of their children or the responsibility of taking care of those children. Often they just hook up with another woman at work or at an evening outing, and they simply walk out on their family. Why? What causes people to do these dreadful and unloving things? How does a parent, male or female, shut off their feelings for their spouse or their children or the things that are best for the family as a whole?

They get out of agreement. They stop loving and giving and forgiving. Selfishness and stubbornness reign in their lives and they refuse to make even the smallest sacrifices for their children. Conflicts rage at every meal. Fathers blame mothers, saying the mothers put the children first. Mothers blame fathers, saying the fathers don't do their part or bring in enough money. Accusations and blame dominate every conversation. In the midst of that conflict, the children get angry and act out defiantly.

Is there any hope once these kinds of wounds have been suffered? Yes. God gave us a blueprint for happy marriages, loving homes and successful children. How can we tap into His grace and mercy and powers of restoration?

First, mothers and fathers have to admit when they are hurting. They have to remember when they loved each other, and how they felt as they waited for the birth of their first little baby. They have to lay down their anger, their pain, and their desire to blame each other. If the mother is hurting and unfulfilled in her marriage, there is a good chance the father is, too. They have to stop, kneel down and give every bit of their pain to Jesus. They have to ask Him to step into their marriage, into the family relationships, into their broken and wounded hearts and minds and cover them with the healing light of His love.

That takes courage. It is not easy to admit you are hurting to someone you want to blame for your pain. It is not easy to expect a change to come over that person, to believe that he or she sincerely wants to put life and health back into the marriage. Many times the only way a couple can let God's healing flow into their lives is to do it for the children.

And it can work. Rebellious teenagers, caught up in all kinds of dangerous and self-destructive behavior, will be forced to stop and rethink everything when they see their parents do a complete turnaround, changing their resentment and bitterness toward each other. There is a lot of power in seeing two people fall to their knees and beg God's forgiveness, when they promise to do whatever it takes to change their ways and to give their all for their family.

God will help such couples get into agreement on all issues. But He will expect them to take action on the things they have promised to do. That will mean no more defending a child, no more covering and protecting and allowing that child to come between the mother and the father. They will have to discuss what each of them expects. They will have to reach a compromise and stick to it.

I heard a story about a father and his son that really made an impression on me. The son got involved in drugs. He worked for his father, in a position of trust. The father found out what was going on, and he had to make a decision. God will give us wisdom if we will simply stop long enough to pray and listen for His reply. In this case, the father was inspired to say the only thing that might have worked. He looked at his son and he said, "I'm not going to give you up. I guess I'll just have to have a man in my organization who uses drugs." That broke the young man's heart. He wept. God had given the father words that brought healing. The son did not want to risk his father's reputation. He did not want to bring disgrace to the family name. Through his father's grace and mercy, the son was able to get control of his life again.

A marriage that is in the process of being healed cannot allow the children to be in control. The parents must identify the areas of conflict and take control of them. How will money be spent in the home? Who will decide the priorities? Power plays have to be eliminated. There can be no hidden issues, no secret agendas and no covering up for a child. Decisions about what the children can and cannot do will have to be made by both parents, and they will have to make it clear that there is no negotiation.

I can say right now that this kind of healing and restructuring of a marriage has a better chance when the children are younger and the severity of the problems is not so great. It takes unbelievable levels of courage and commitment to achieve a renewed marriage when there are older teenagers involved, and they are deeply into rebellion and trouble. But it can be done. There is no situation beyond our God.

Children are meant to be a joy. They can bring fulfillment, satisfaction and the utmost pleasure to us as we grow older. *"Children's children are a crown to the aged, and parents are the pride of their children"* Proverbs 17:6, NIV.

"They are always generous and lend freely; their children will be

blessed" Psalms 37:26, NIV.

"His children will be mighty in the land; the generation of the upright will be blessed" Psalms 112:2, NIV.

"Sons are a heritage from the LORD, children a reward from him" Psalms 127:3, NIV.

It is time we teach our children to value biblical family principles. It's time we raise them to understand God has expectations about family relationships. We need to make it a practice in the body of Christ to support new parents, to offer young families the advice gained through experience, to shore them up when they hit parenting bumps, to stand in the gap for them and to keep our young families and our teenagers in constant prayer.

Parents who want to keep the honey in their honeymoons cannot sacrifice that sweetness to rebellious, materialistic, or manipulative children. They must establish goals and parenting philosophies and make *agreement* an unshakable standard in their homes.

That is the only way our sweet and innocent young couple we met at the beginning of this chapter will be able to raise their child in confidence and see that child through to adulthood, while maintaining the strength and love God intended for them to enjoy inside their marriage.

Children come to go. That is a fact that husbands and wives need to understand. It is the normal and natural progression of life that our children grow up, leave us, marry and form their own families. That is another reason that the marriage relationship must be nurtured, cultivated and lovingly developed.

Every time I hear a couple that is concerned about having an "empty nest," I smile. They are about to embark on one of the sweetest parts of marriage. When children leave, parents can rediscover the joys of privacy, the intimacy of a second honeymoon, and the thrill of focusing all their attention on each other again. And trust me, parents who reach this point will forever understand the expression, *"Saving the best for last."*

Chapter 8

A Bed of Roses

I can't write a book about keeping the honey in the honeymoon without talking about the intimacy issues in marriage. And intimacy involves so much more than sex! Sex is a part of marriage. As we said earlier, God even instructed husbands and wives not to deny sex to each other. "*Let the husband render to his wife the affection due her, and likewise also the wife to her husband. The wife does not have authority over her own body, but the husband does. And likewise the husband does not have authority over his own body, but the wife does. Do not deprive one another except with consent for a time, that you may give yourselves to fasting and prayer; and come together again so that Satan does not tempt you because of your lack of self-control* 1 Corinthians 7: 3-5, Amplified.

But if intimacy is more than sex, what is it? I think it is the familiarity and communication in the shared looks that a husband and wife give each other, looks that convey love, a memory, a warning, and all the other emotions and protections they have in their experience banks. Intimacy is a hand on a knee or back, a quick touch to convey support, affection, or compassion. Intimacy is the message a husband or wife can convey across a crowded room, a silent "*I love you*" or "*Let's go home.*"

Intimacy precedes the sex act. It is the silent or spoken, physical and mental contact that makes a husband and wife long to be together. If the only intimacy a couple experiences is in the bed, they are not having true intimacy. They are having sex. No more and no less. They are missing out on all the pleasures, closeness and rewards that come from a loving, giving, committed marriage relationship.

Couples who are truly in love are blessed beyond description.

Each of them has a best friend, a lover, a confidant, a financial partner, a parenting partner, and a safe harbor from life's storms. Does such a relationship happen naturally? No. Remember when we talked about the devil's plans for our marriages? The enemy's goal is to derail as many couples as possible, to make people think good marriages are a myth, to tempt, cheat and waylay people and make certain they never attain the ultimate benefits from marriage.

Why? Because there is power in agreement. If a husband and wife attain the level of love and satisfaction God intended them to reach in their relationship, they will have a powerful influence over others. Good marriages are obvious. I can see them in my church, recognize them when I look out over my congregation. These are the people I call on to pray for others. These are the people I know will be strongest when it comes to standing in the gap for others, praying with them and over them, and interceding on their behalf.

How is this level of love and affection achieved? How is it that some people understand the concept of two becoming one, while others resist it to their detriment? I'm not really sure. But I do have eyes to see and ears to hear, and I can relate the things that are present in good marriages.

Good marriages are places where the husband and wife *both* value the other more than they value themselves. They heed the Scripture that says, *"Be kindly affectioned one to another with brotherly love; in honour preferring one another..."* Romans 12:10, KJV.

That is not always easy to do. But once a husband and wife begin to experience the fruit that comes from such behavior, they realize its value. Love is expressed in every encounter a husband and wife have throughout the day. The tone of voice they use on the phone. The kisses that say hello and good-bye. The meals that are prepared, the little chores performed and all the other expressions that say, *"You are important to me."*

I have talked to many people who have beautiful marriages. I have a wonderful marriage myself. Are there secrets to a good marriage? Absolutely. Is it possible for anyone to attain that kind of relationship? It is. Easily? No. Because being a good husband or a good wife means putting your spouse first, turning your back on the things the world says you have a "right" to, and trusting another person to honor you and reward your sacrifices.

There are so many things that go into a good marriage: never putting the children first, making sure you schedule 'alone time,' special dinners for two, vacations, back rubs and massages, hand-holding, long walks, avoiding going to bed angry, refusing to take offense, going on frequent 'dates,' cards, thoughtful little gifts, kind words, small surprises, and lots of sex. That's just the beginning. But any marriage where both partners make a commitment to supply the above needs can be fairly certain it will succeed.

Several years ago, a Christian woman wrote a book where she advocated meeting the husband at the door in a sexy outfit and basically fulfilling all his fantasies. I can't even remember the name of the book, it's been so long, but there was a lot of criticism, and joking about it in Christian circles.

That's too bad. She gave good advice. It's a hard cruel world. I know many wives who love to surprise their husbands with special dinners. They plan them down to the smallest details, selecting his favorite foods, making sure the children will be away for the evening, setting a beautiful table, lighting candles, playing soft music and generally creating an atmosphere where he will feel very special.

People in the work force are often under a great deal of stress, both husbands and wives. Thankfully, we live in a society that is much more sensitive to the balance of labor in the home. If the husband happens to be the one at home with an opportunity to provide such a beautiful dinner, more power to him. The important thing is the evening, the special nature of it, and the intimacy the couple will share. Not *who* prepares it.

Couples need to feel free to simply adore each other. If you have a song that meant something very special to you and your spouse when you were dating, you should remember to play it now and then. You might dance cheek to cheek, and lose yourselves in the feelings that made you love each other in the first place.

Atmosphere is important. A crackling fire on a cold night, lots of candles and special desserts. These are things that make a great evening even more wonderful. I know one couple that lines the edge of their hot tub with candles. They play soft music and they share the events of the day or the last few days. They do this almost every night. Just enjoying the luxury of time together, relaxing in the churning hot water and letting all the stresses of the day give way as they enjoy their sanctuary.

A couple that has just had this experience is not going to go upstairs and do battle over the mortgage payment, or about who left the towel on the floor or squeezed the toothpaste tube in the middle. They will be feeling mellow. Maybe they'll take the soft music inside with them, and they will continue their intimacy and their pleasure in each other's company.

This could be a great time for a massage, first one and then the other. It's a good time for back rubs, and it is a bad time for television! No evening news should enter into this scene. Stress begets stress. The stock report will still be available in the morning. The negative news the media has to offer will be splashed all over the front page of tomorrow's newspaper.

The world has many designs on our time, our views, and our money. The last thing they want is for us to be content in each other's company, laughing and loving, with no television to parade the many products they want us to think we have to have in order to be happy.

Time alone is a big gift. When your spouse turns off the television set, lays down that book, or turns off the computer and says, "What would you like to do?" that is an important offering. Don't pick up the remote control, flip to some silly program and say, "Aw, nothing. Let's just watch TV."

At the end of the week or the month, I doubt that anyone ever says, "I wish I'd watched more television." I've never encountered a single person on the deathbed who regretted the sitcoms they'd missed or the soap operas they failed to watch. No, what people regret at the end of life is the time they failed to spend with loved ones, or the degree to which they gave themselves to their marriages.

The Power of Intimacy

It is important to acknowledge your spouse's touch. Sometimes I will hear a man complain that when he touches or tries to kiss his wife, she turns away. Maybe the children are in the room. So what? What better example can we give our children than teaching them husbands and wives kiss, they love each other and consider each other important? Obviously, I am talking about keeping things in proper and decent order here. But a kiss is a good thing for a child to see. Love between parents assures a child that the world is safe and secure for the moment.

I have heard wives say the reason they turn away from their husbands is because they fear the kiss or the touch will lead to sexual intimacy, and they have too much to do at that time. That may be valid. So husbands and wives need to get into *agreement* that a kiss is just a kiss with no hidden agenda. When the wife trusts and believes that her husband sincerely wants to kiss her, she may become more demonstrative herself.

The danger of turning away the husband's kiss should be obvious. No one likes rejection. It hurts. And if she didn't want his kiss at 5:30 in the evening, he might decide he doesn't want to kiss her when they go to bed. This kind of behavior escalates in a hurry. She begins to think he only wants to touch her if they are going to have sex. She suspects every kiss and every pat on the back or the bottom. She's distrustful and defensive. He quits trying. Before long, they find themselves in a physical standoff. Nothing is spontaneous or natural. They stop being playful and loving. Time passes, and they begin to buy into that false idea that they are too old or too serious for sexual intimacy.

Real danger can come into their bedroom at this point. Human urges being what they are, they will still occasionally have sex. But it can become automatic and practiced. And that's not even the end of the downward spiral their relationship can take. As I've said, this is what the devil has been after all along. Their marriage!

This is the time when pornography enters many homes. Because the couple is not being affectionate and spontaneous on a daily basis, because their lovemaking is more lust than love, they begin to think they need some extra stimulation. Speaking in generalities, men probably like pornography better than women. Women usually feel guilty about it sooner and have a more instinctive sense of how degrading it really is. But even men eventually feel repelled by watching dirty movies or reading pornography before or during sex.

Both of them will begin to remember a time when they could get excited and sexually aroused without resorting to pornography. And because their consciences have been so seared by all they have seen, experienced, and reacted to, they may begin to imagine themselves with other sexual partners, hoping to recreate those earlier levels of stimulation.

Sin is progressive. One act leads to another and then another. A seared conscience can no longer protect and warn. Once a couple has engaged in sexual acts while stimulated by pornography, while fantasizing they are with other people, it is a short and almost inevitable step to adultery.

The Bible warns us clearly about these things. *"The acts of the sinful nature are obvious: sexual immorality, impurity and debauchery; idolatry and witchcraft; hatred, discord, jealousy, fits of rage, selfish ambition, dissensions, factions and envy; drunkenness, orgies, and the like"* Galatians 5:19-21, NIV.

I suppose it isn't even necessary to talk about the loss of respect a husband and wife feel for each other once they get involved with this level of sin. I have heard husbands who felt it was all right for them to get caught up with pornography because they were 'men,' but who sincerely felt they could no longer stay with their wives because they had participated.

Pornography is evil. It takes people prisoner, and it destroys an individual's love for spouse, marriage, and self. It causes much worse than the destruction of marriages in this world, but that's not the topic this book is meant to address. Christians should stay as far from pornography as possible. They cannot and should not support any part of an industry that defiles, enslaves, humiliates and destroys human beings. And certainly, pornography has no place in a Christian home where parents are charged to set a good example of God's love for their children.

We have talked about husbands and wives enjoying nice meals and time alone. We have discussed the importance of physical contact and touching. There are other things couples can do to promote closeness. Married people need to go on 'dates.' They need to plan surprises and special events, to look forward to and initiate creative outings. I've noticed something about 'dating' husbands and wives. When he is making the plans, the husband has a tendency to get tickets to the theater or a concert or something else he knows his wife will enjoy. When she is making the plans, she'll choose a sporting event or an action movie, the kinds of things she thinks will be special to him. Isn't that wonderful? By the very nature of planning a date, one spouse automatically looks for a way to bless the other.

Money helps when planning this kind of entertainment, but it is not necessary. Young couples usually have so many places where their money needs to go that if they waited to save enough for a big fancy evening, they would never go on a date. These evenings don't have to be expensive. Maybe a husband could plan a wonderful surprise picnic at a lake where they first met, or a wife could create a luau or a beach trip in the backyard! Sometimes I think those kinds of dates are the best. It takes a lot of effort to make the backyard look like the South Pacific or to make a trip to the local lake seem like an evening on a Hawaiian beach.

Music, pictures, blankets, posters, a roaring campfire and other accessories can make a spectacular success out of something ordinary. It's the effort that makes an impression. No husband or wife could fail to be moved by a special day or evening planned and carried out with such a high level of creativity.

There are so many small and inexpensive things that can bring love and caring out in a spouse. Greeting cards. Notes. Tiny, but meaningful gifts left in the driver's seat before a husband or wife leaves for work, or on a pillow just before bedtime can mean so much. My husband travels a lot, so I try to pack little notes and gifts into his suitcase, sometimes one for each day he'll be away. I make a lipstick 'kiss' for him and tell him that I love him. I let him know I'm thinking about him. These kinds of things don't have to cost a lot of money. Handmade gifts and homemade cards are wonderful.

We've covered several ways that a couple can enrich their marriage and add to the fulfillment they experience. Imagine how children would thrive in such a home. Some families go through so many arguments and power plays that the children feel like survivors from a war zone.

No one has to live like that! It's true. The world doesn't want us to believe that bit of information. They like their court systems, and medical buildings filled with psychiatrists, child behavior specialists, and counselors, and their countless advocates and attorneys and recovery clinics. Those things may work for a while, maybe in extreme or abusive situations, but by and large, they do not help people find the fulfillment and joy that come from good family relationships and successful marriages.

People have to want to succeed at marriage. It helps to choose a spouse who also wants to succeed. But even when both husband and wife come from homes where arguments, power plays and divorce were common, they can find victory. How? By reading the Bible and fashioning their marriage after God's blueprint. Get into agreement about finances, childrearing, authority, and intimacy. Be faithful in a local church, associate with Christian families who understand the dynamics of a godly home.

If possible, you and your spouse should try to get away once in a while, away from home, away from children, away from jobs and phones and chores. This doesn't have to be for a long time, and it doesn't have to be a trip halfway around the world. Many hotels offer spectacular weekend packages for one or two nights that include one very nice dinner, continental breakfasts and time in their pools and spas. It is amazing how refreshing a weekend like that can be for a couple.

Longer, more elaborate vacations can come later, once the children are a bit older. My point is that just being young, on a budget, and the parents of tiny children should not be an excuse for any couple to neglect their 'alone' time. It's nice to have friends, other couples you share common interests with, but being alone is sometimes better.

Husbands and wives who are serious about having a great marriage will adopt the behaviors we've talked about. They will look forward to surprising their spouse with a note or a card or a small gift. They will plan getaways and dates and short vacations. They will cook something special, create a wonderful evening, buy a song or a CD that has special meaning, and they will always seek that extra touch that will melt their spouse's heart. They will cherish time alone and make it so wonderful that their spouse will start trying to think of ways to return the favor.

Try to keep your bedroom attractive and comfortable. Remember that spending quality time together will never work well when the television set is playing. In fact, the bedroom will be happier if the television set doesn't dominate the room and command all the attention. The Word says, *"Let all things be done decently and in order"* 1 Corinthians 14:40, KJV. Keeping a television set in the bedroom is all right (especially for very busy couples) as long as both husband and wife remember that it is not the only entertainment in the room.

Watch your wedding video once in a while or look through your wedding album together. You might even want to read your marriage vows again or, better yet, write new ones that reflect your more mature love, and repeat those vows for the children or just for each other.

Promise not to pick up offenses and let your feelings be hurt over anything. What she said may not mean what a tired husband thinks, or a wife who has been talking to two-year-olds all day can easily misinterpret a comment about her hair or her make-up. When two people love each other, they have to learn to laugh at such comments and to understand their marriage is more than a moment, more than an out-of-context remark. Remind each other once in a while that the devil wants you to fail. He wants you arguing and yelling and crying, scaring your babies, throwing dishes and running home to Mama.

He really does. And he cannot stand it when you have joy in your hearts, when you cannot wait to be back together at the end of the day. Never go to sleep until you have reached agreement and resolution over an issue. Going to sleep angry can mean going to sleep without a kiss, without saying, "I love you."

When couples do that, the devil slips right into the situation. "See?" he says. "She doesn't care. She doesn't appreciate all you've done. And about that hug. Why doesn't she want one? What has she been up to?" And to the wife, he whispers, "He doesn't kiss you because you don't look half as pretty as the women he works with all day. You don't need him. What's he hiding from anyway?"

Those kinds of attacks happen to couples; it will happen to someone tonight. Pride and the fear of rejection can cause husbands and wives to fall asleep brokenhearted and without expressing their deep love. And because the devil is so crafty, the very thing the couple fears will soon come to pass. Because the moment they stop protecting their marriage with *agreement,* the enemy steps in to sabotage it with disharmony.

I am convinced that the way we respond to offense is what determines our futures. If we choose to be offended and pout and whine until we get our way, we will pay a terrible price over the years. Like the smoker who wants a cigarette more than he or she fears the physical repercussions, the person who cherishes the right to be offended may be blindly choosing the death of their marriage.

Choose life. Protect the marriage bed. Make it a happy place where both husband and wife are eager to go. Sexual satisfaction is a good thing. It is a scriptural thing. It keeps people calm and loving and it also keeps them from making foolish choices out of need and frustration. Many marriages that could have been saved, that *should* have been saved, lie buried under pride, arrogance, and stubbornness.

Love is a wonderful thing. A trusted spouse is a treasured friend. Our moments together need to be cherished. Our private times should be guarded and protected like the great riches they are.

As I said, children come to go. The thing we need to hold most dear, the thing we need to pamper and protect above all other treasures, is the marriage relationship.

Part III

Be Ready for Anything!

Chapter 9

Ignore Everything the World has to Say

This bit of advice can save your marriage from a lot of grief. This chapter may seem irrelevant to some, an unnecessary warning. It is not. The world exerts unbelievable pressure every day to get people's trust and allegiance. This book is not part of a crusade to attack everything in modern society. But there is a saying that states, "Garbage in, garbage out." We have to assume responsibility for the things we take into our hearts, our minds and our spirits. The Word says, *"Above all else, guard your heart, for it is the wellspring of life"* Proverbs 4:23, NIV.

"May the words of my mouth and the meditation of my heart be pleasing in your sight, O LORD, my Rock and my Redeemer" Psalms 19:14, NIV.

Secular society has a jaded view of marriage. Hollywood is well known for its short, publicity-driven weddings, its high-profile divorces, and an overriding cynicism for the marriage institution. Because so many stars and executives in the entertainment industry have had negative personal experiences, they seem determined to portray those views in much of their work. Misery loves company. And perhaps, because of their life experiences, they sincerely believe all marriage relationships are as bad as the ones they have had.

I'm reminded of the Oscar-winning film, American Beauty. It was a celebration of marital dysfunction, drug abuse, pedophilia, infidelity and murder. People told me they left the theater perplexed, shaking their heads, and wondering whose idea of reality had created that storyline. But conversely, people who were interviewed, people who actually voted for the Oscar awards, universally applauded the movie for its gritty truths and its honest portrayals.

That is why I am urging families to ignore everything the world has to say about marriage! Should we trust people who think all husbands and fathers are lusting after their daughter's young friends, who think it is all right and even humorous when Mom goes off to work every morning, but she's actually having an affair with her boss, who support a movie that says our youngsters are drug-dealing addicts who stalk and spy and generally display the behavior we once associated with hardened criminals? Have we reached a point in our society where murder is thought to be a happy ending?

We cannot trust the world's solutions for marriages. Its motives, track record, and sincerity are all suspect. God gave us a wonderful blueprint for our lives and our homes, while the world opted to take every reference to God out of public schools. We have political leaders and people in positions of power and influence who have lied under oath, defiled buildings and offices that were once honored, and who have chosen to give America's young people the worst possible example of what husbands, wives and parents should be.

How can we teach morality to young men and women when it seems the church is standing all alone on a battleground for accountability and high standards? How can we explain that infidelity and lying are wrong, that they will destroy homes, marriages and families, when our youngsters see people in very high places get away with those things? Do we want our children to believe that all politicians lie? Do we want them to get the idea that corruption and dishonesty are more common than nobility and truth?

No. We must continue to teach, give good examples, and believe with all our hearts that there is a remnant of God's people that will once again have influence and authority in this land. We must stand firm, hold the line, and resist present trends, because we know God will not be mocked forever.

What the World Honors

The world's values are clear. Look at its heroes. Look at advertising. Look at the influence and respect the world gives people simply because they have a lot of money. God knew that temptation would be there for all of us. In Matthew 6:24, we read, "*No one can serve two masters. Either he will hate the one and love the other, or he will be devoted to the one and despise the other. You cannot serve both God and Money*" NIV. But certainly, many try to do just that.

In addition to its love for money, I've noticed the world loves competition. It loves sporting events, spelling bees, geography contests and television quiz shows. It honors the best, the prettiest, the thinnest, the smartest, the richest, and the wildest, often idolizing heroes and heroines, following them with cameras, entertaining them on talk shows, and showering them with adoration and respect. Why? What criteria are we using to judge people?

Appearance, success, athletic skill, physical dominance, and talent. Our society is fickle, moving from the admiration of one entertainer or sports team to the next. We have best-dressed lists, whose hot and whose not, most beautiful lists, sexiest lists, and of course, The Man of the Year.

I mention all of these individuals, these icons who dominate the airwaves, books and Internet, to say this: Most of these people have done nothing to earn our respect. They have not lived lives that we should try to emulate. We need to make sure our young people are not silently worshipping some sports hero or rock star or rapper who is a poor role model. We need to monitor the things our children watch, listen to and respect. We need to ask them what they know about that person's life, their beliefs, and their values.

Parents, grandparents, Sunday school teachers, pastors and youth leaders can talk all day about godly homes, good marriages, sexual accountability, and moral righteousness, but if they do not monitor young people's activities, if they do not ask questions and raise important ethical issues, they will not win the day.

Peers and role models and generational attitudes are very powerful. Young people always seem to strive for an image that fits their decade. When we think of the 20s, we think of flappers. The 30s were dominated by the depression and kids who had to work hard. The 40s remind us of World War II, young soldiers, and women who got their first real taste of individuality and independence. The 50s were Happy Days and perhaps the beginning of the child generations. The 60s, revolution and freethinking—flower children. The 70s gave us double-knits and the Brady Bunch. The 80s and the 90s were times when more and more liberal thinking began to dominate, and immorality was celebrated rather than condemned.

So what will we face in this new millennium? There's an abundance of music, dancing and young rock stars. I don't know that I disapprove of modern music, but the biggest reason is I can't understand the lyrics. I listen. I've been told many of the words are dangerous and negative. So parents have to find out what their children are listening to. They have to understand the words or read the lyric sheets that come with many CD's. We cannot let television, computers, radios and music babysit our young people.

What's wrong with television? Believe it or not, I have been asked that question by Christian parents. They point to the educational qualities of television, to programming for tiny children that promotes learning and stimulates their thinking. Some of that is good. It's wonderful to broaden their understanding in areas of medicine, the animal kingdom, Christianity, education, cooking and other helpful topics.

But there is a lot of programming that is bad. Television dramas and sit-coms have often been faulted for solving all problems in a thirty or sixty minute segment. That's a valid complaint. We have people (many of them parents themselves) who grew up with the idea that all troubles could be solved in less than an hour.

This kind of thinking has generated a lot of problems. Our attention spans seem shorter. People are easily agitated when traffic jams, lines at the bank or the grocery store, long waits for doctor appointments, and other delays slow them down. They are accustomed to instant gratification. People get shot on cartoons and they pop back up, alive and well. Children are constantly exposed to a television world where injuries have no lasting repercussions, and every roadblock, disease and setback is remedied in a few minutes and three or four commercials.

Television life pretends to be real. Real families. Real marriages. Real people cast away on desert islands. Real millionaires who simply have to have fast enough fingers and answers to win their way to the top of the quest for cash. But television life is not real! Viewers can't see the cameras, the dressing rooms, the make-up people and all the other equipment.

So if television families are not real, if their problems are simply scripted and made to fit inside a certain time frame, why would we try to fashion our lives and our problem solving after them? Television deals with marriage and divorce in a careless way, discarding spouses with little regard, bringing entire second and third families into programs with casual ease. Why wouldn't young viewers decide that infidelity, living together before marriage, and pre-marital sex were all perfectly acceptable choices?

In real life it is difficult to build successful second marriages, to blend families and deal with the challenges of stepchildren, half-siblings, non-custodial parents and all the other relationships that challenge modern society. And when extended families don't turn out to be cute and easy and successful like they are on television, many people get discouraged. They think they have done something wrong, that perhaps they have failed again, and they wonder if they should just give up.

They shouldn't. Marriages, even second and third marriages, involve vows and commitments. What people fail to learn the first time is certain to come around and challenge them again. And I have learned in counseling that it is easier to give up the second or the third time. It is easier to walk away. And why wouldn't it be? It happens in movies and on television all the time.

In spite of the popularity of divorce, people feel guilty when they fail at marriage. They may justify it in their minds and when they talk to others, but divorce isn't fun. Broken families leave bleeding and wounded children, and they leave bleeding and wounded adults.

It isn't funny like the stand-up comics make it sound. In real life divorce is rarely friendly, and it doesn't usually involve sophisticated adults who happily adjust to joint custody, delightful visits back and forth and a sense that all is well in the world. Real life divorce creates ex-spouses who feel like failures. Their self-esteem nose-dives, and the chances that they will eventually achieve a happy and fulfilling marriage go way down.

We have to stop getting our ideas about life and how we should live it from television programs and movies. The motives for these offerings are all wrong. They're based on ratings and on what the most dedicated couch potatoes want to see. Fake happiness sells as well as fake murder and violence, which sells as well as sporting events. Sexual promiscuity and illicit affairs are both popular programming plots.

But sexual promiscuity does not generate the same negative results on TV that it does in real life. If people form their opinions about the consequences of sexual misconduct from what they see on television, they will be in for a bitter surprise when they mimic those kinds of choices.

They never really deal with infants born out of wedlock on thirty-minute sitcoms. And if they did, the subject would be treated as whimsical, triumphant and lighthearted, refusing to focus on real life problems like child support, daycare, and the difficulty single mothers have raising a child alone.

When we look at actors, we need to remember their flaws are covered up by special lenses and camera angles. They don't take their imaginary 'families' home with them at night. In fact, they have to leave the clothing, the wigs and often the bubbly personalities behind when they leave the studio. So why, knowing it is all fantasy, do so many people try to pattern their lifestyles after the characters they see on the screen?

What are the motives for television and movie portrayals of life? Why do they persistently feature slender, childlike women who act out sexually but who have all the mannerisms of pre-teen girls? Why do they portray aging men as handsome, charming and successful and portray aging women as critical, harsh and bitter? They are catering to stereotypes. In other words, they are giving viewers what they *think* they want.

Programming decisions are based on what advertisers want to sell. We've all seen products appear onscreen, consumed, worn or used by characters, and we don't think anything about it. But we've just seen a commercial. Young people are particularly vulnerable to wanting the products they see people using on television. Ever wonder why Saturday morning programming for children is so popular with advertisers? Because children exert tremendous pressure to get the things they want.

Does anyone seriously believe the latest rash of animated films were carefully screened for their interest levels and appropriateness for children? Can we honestly say we thought *The Hunchback of Notre Dame* was appropriate fiction for toddlers? Or *Anna and the King of Siam?* Or *Pocahontas?* I think these stories were selected for their merchandising value: Action figures, fast food meals for children, T-shirts, glassware, puzzles, bedding, etc.

Advertising is the generator behind programming and content. It is safe to say that biblical standards, moral values, accountability and repercussions for poor choices will never be prominently featured on most network media. Not only do they say it won't sell—they don't want it to sell. Immorality is more popular than morality. Sin appears to be a lot more fun than living a well-stewarded life. Good stewards do not spend the family income on tobacco, alcohol, and other vices that advertisers constantly market.

The advertising industry tries to manipulate people. When they have something they want to sell, they simply tell everyone it's already trendy. They have all the most admired television and movie stars wear it, or drive it or eat it. They create their own fads. People are often so gullible and so determined to be seen eating, wearing and driving the 'right' thing that they buy right into the fake fad.

In addition to promoting poor moral and life choices, the media loves to promote rivalry and a sense that we cannot slow down for a minute or we will lose our edge, our position or our chance to be a success. There is a relentless barrage of programming and advertising that encourages a sense of competition and aggressive positioning.

What is the point? Money. People who are jockeying for positions of power based on their income, their home, the clothes they wear, the car they drive or the places where they vacation, will be more willing to spend every cent they make on enhancing their status. They will select restaurants, theaters, clothing, neighborhoods and even their spouse, based on a standard that has no real merit.

And don't think for one minute that being in a church protects people from shallow values. Some of the most shocking examples of being house-proud, car-proud and clothes-proud can be found in churches today. I have been in big facilities where name brand clothing, name brand electronics and name brand cars were given more attention than the message preached.

It is vitally important in these challenging times to make certain you do not let national media influence your family, relationships, and choices. Television and movies are not the only dangers. Don't forget the Internet, which has gained enormous power in a very short time. I think it is safe to say it may end up being the single biggest challenge to good parenting that couples will face in this generation.

The Internet is exploding. It is filled with good things. Great things. Its educational value has never been equaled. Students and researchers can find more resources and information there than anywhere else on earth. It has leveled the playing field in many areas. People seeking facts and information have the equivalent of all the world's great libraries right at the tip of their fingers!

That is awesome. Many versions of the Bible are available, as well as great concordances, biblical research and an endless array of books.

Obscure studies and facts are offered to people all over the earth. This is the greatest blessing ever imagined for people dedicated to fulfilling the Great Commission.

"Therefore go and make disciples of all nations, baptizing them in the name of the Father and of the Son and of the Holy Spirit, and teaching them to obey everything I have commanded you. And surely I am with you always, to the very end of the age" Matthew 28:19-20, NIV.

It is also one of the greatest tools the devil has ever had the opportunity to corrupt, influence and use to take control of people's lives. The excess of pornography online has shocked even those people who support it. Because abusers change screen names, steal passwords, and illegally send their smut to millions of unsuspecting users, they make a lot of money.

Many young people have been lured into this terrible environment by simply opening a message claiming to be from another young person. There is nothing right or fair or truthful about the people who commit these crimes. They are smart, fast and evil. They do not care whose credit card a youngster uses; they do not care how young the people are that they victimize.

But, believe it or not, the pornographers aren't the biggest danger on the Internet. The worst people are the opportunistic pedophiles who constantly monitor conversations in chat rooms, who send out instant messages, and who will do anything to befriend young people. These individuals love the secrecy of the Internet, the fact they can't be seen. They hold long conversations with children, opportunities where they learn a great deal about their victims as they groom them and lure them with gifts.

We need to monitor our children's time on the Internet. We need to make them understand that it is just like a big city. It has wonderful cultural opportunities, educational treasures and deep spiritual truths. But like cities, it has dangerous areas, places where crimes occur and where people are often victimized.

Some people are afraid the Internet is hopelessly corrupt. They don't want to see if the greater good or the greater evil prevails in the end. But we have to remember, we've read the end of the Book. We win. Computers are one of the greatest evangelical tools ever placed in Christians' hands. But computers are machines. We have to use them with caution, and we must always be aware that the enemy would love to steal this technology from us.

Setting Our Own Standards

Another area where we have to exercise caution is the print media. Books are magnificent tools. So are magazines. John and I believe they are wonderful ways to reach people and convey a message.

But the print media can also reflect the attitudes, recommendations, and political leanings of their major advertisers. For example, do not look for a newspaper to give fair and impartial campaign coverage. They will lean to the left or to the right. I have heard that when a newspaper is about to drop their endorsement of a political candidate, they use a different photo file for any pictures they print of that individual. Those photographs are generally unflattering, pictures where the candidate looks exhausted, eyes drooping, mouth hanging open. Is that fair? Certainly not. We need to realize the news is slanted and that all reporting has a certain amount of bias.

Earlier I talked about the push for competition in the media, the idea that we are all in a race for success, publicity and fame. Media sources have us constantly examining our lives, our possessions, our educations, and our families to see if we measure up. We really need to resist those kinds of comparisons.

Let's just imagine a newly married couple. What if they constantly compared each other to the characters they saw on television shows? Real life husbands and wives don't have witty lines written for them every day. They get tired. Sometimes they don't feel well. There is no way they will measure up to characters who have makeup artists, extensive wardrobes and special lighting to make them look good.

When we first fall in love, everything about our beloved seems perfect. The Song of Solomon gives us a wonderful example of that. *"My lover is radiant and ruddy, outstanding among ten thousand. His head is purest gold; his hair is wavy and black as a raven. His eyes are like doves by the water streams, washed in milk, mounted like jewels. His cheeks are like beds of spice yielding perfume. His lips are like lilies dripping with myrrh. His arms are rods of gold set with chrysolite. His body is like polished ivory decorated with sapphires. His legs are pillars of marble set on bases of pure gold. His appearance is like Lebanon, choice as its cedars. His mouth is sweetness itself; he is altogether lovely. This is my lover, this my friend, O daughters of Jerusalem"* Song of Solomon 5:10-17, NIV.

So what happens when his beloved grows used to him? When she begins to compare him to others she's seen in the marketplace? Comparison is dangerous. It is unrealistic. We can't judge people by appearances. What we see is not always all there is to a story. Why? Where does that drive to create an illusion come from? Often it's born out of that old familiar tendency we discussed in an earlier chapter—the "What-will-people-think?" spirit. Couples who operate their marriages on that principle are masters at the art of deception. They are like homemakers I've known who have spotless houses, but when dresser drawers, cupboards and closets are opened, all the hidden trash tumbles out.

Because appearances can be deceiving, comparisons are never valid. Neither is it valid to take all those silly truth tests, happy marriage tests, compatibility tests, and other kinds of quizzes that are so popular in women's magazines and on daytime talk shows. There are too many variables, too many unknowns, to make these tests work correctly.

We have to ask ourselves, "What is the motive for this test? Does the author have a political agenda? Is he/she twisting statistics to make a point? Is it a sales pitch?" We all need to be better fruit inspectors! What is the fruit of the magazine? What is the fruit of the television show we are watching? Or the network? Who profits? Is the show highly publicized in order to attract viewers or sell more of the sponsor's wares?

The secular world has an agenda for almost everything it does. Because of that, they do not offer valid strategies and plans for happy marriages. They have all kinds of remedies in place for failure; they have safe houses, prisons and divorce courts—but they don't have answers for people who do not want to join the endless parade of shattered husbands and wives and the vast army of hurting and disillusioned children.

Ask people if the Bible should be the standard we use in our homes, and they will laugh and joke and shake their heads. Ask them if the Ten Commandments should be taught in schools, and they will think that is an offensive and politically incorrect idea. But ask them if they think children should be taught that stealing is bad. Ask them if they think children need to have a greater sense of respect and love for their parents and other adults in authority. The truth is most people believe these are good values to have, good things to teach children. But they are so brain washed by the media that they refuse to admit we've replaced the Bible with babble.

We live in a world where many unchurched people have influence in our lives. The Word says, *"They are from the world and therefore speak from the viewpoint of the world, and the world listens to them. We are from God, and whoever knows God listens to us; but whoever is not from God does not listen to us. This is how we recognize the Spirit of truth and the spirit of falsehood"* 1 John 4: 5-6, NIV.

That is a really good word for us. It makes it clear that these challenges we face are not new. They will almost certainly face Christian families until Jesus returns. That is why people mock Christian families and refuse to believe that our marriages and our ways of bringing up our young people are better. *"We are from God, and whoever knows God listens to us; but whoever is not from God does not listen to us..."* Remember how God hardened Pharaoh's heart so no matter what Moses said to him about letting his people go, he couldn't hear?

That's how this is. The world has a different agenda. We think we can just tell them how living life by God's blueprint works, how it frees people from debt, creates strong and happy marriages, releases people from the bondage of alcohol and addiction, how it teaches ways to raise healthy, happy children and how it brings peace and fulfillment to our days. *"But people who aren't Christians can't understand these truths from God's Spirit. It all sounds foolish to them because only those who have the Spirit can understand what the Spirit means"* 1 Corinthians 2:14, TLB.

They can't hear us. Why? Because they are not God's people. Not yet. And maybe they will choose to turn from God all the days of their lives. We can take them the message. We can perform our part of the Great Commission. But we cannot make them listen. And when they refuse to hear us, we cannot let them steal the honey from our honeymoons. We cannot sacrifice our standards, our morals or the members of our families to them.

The world does not have answers for our marriages. They want to lure us, tempt us, and conform us to their beliefs. Be discerning about the things the world offers. John always says, "Birds can fly over our heads, but we don't have to let them build nests in our hair." We do not have to eat every carrot the world dangles in front of us. We can use the watermelon principle, eating the melon and spitting out the seeds. When it comes to marriage, stick with the Manual. Trust the Master.

Chapter 10

Attacks Will Come—Be Ready

Once we make up our minds to establish godly homes and marriages, the devil jumps into our lives with both feet. See, he does not care that we go to church or that we read the Word or even that we believe. What he cares about, what drives him crazy and forces him into action is when we begin to *do* the things we learn from the Word, when we begin to live life the way God instructed.

Anyone can read the Bible. People can say they are living and acting a certain way, and they will fool others for a season. There are people who regularly attend church that pastors have learned to call "church-smart," people who say all the right things and seem as if they are the most dedicated Christians in the world. But what is the fruit of their lives? A tree is known by its fruit. And so are people. It's easy to talk the talk. But to walk the walk, we have to be filled with the Holy Spirit.

The Word says, *"Anyone who listens to the word but does not do what it says is like a man who looks at his face in a mirror and, after looking at himself, goes away and immediately forgets what he looks like. But the man who looks intently into the perfect law that gives freedom, and continues to do this, not forgetting what he has heard, but doing it—he will be blessed in what he does"* James 1:23-25, NIV.

Understanding this, we can see why it upsets the enemy when we learn to live our lives, establish our marriages, and love each other as God taught. It is at that point, that moment when he realizes he may lose us after all, that he intensifies his attacks. And he has so many tricks, strategies, and methods.

One of his favorite tricks, once people have vowed to turn their lives around and live according to God's plan, is to come against them in their finances. Things break in the house. Unexpected bills, taxes, car repairs and medical expenses occur. This can be extreme, with events coming one right after the other, causing people to doubt God's love, His mercy and His promises. But God's Word is true. In Numbers 23:19, we read, *"God is not a man, that he should lie, nor a son of man, that he should change his mind. Does he speak and then not act? Does he promise and not fulfill"* NIV?

I remember in the late seventies when I began to press into the Word of God. I wanted all that God had for me. It was at that time that John and I began to get the revelation that God wanted to prosper us. The truth was becoming alive and real to us.

The enemy became frightened as we started to walk in these truths: *"...and to put on the new self, created to be like God in true righteousness and holiness"* Ephesians 4:24, NIV. *"I am come that they might have life, and that they might have it more abundantly"* John 10:10, KJV.

That's when the attack started. One major appliance after another broke down: The air conditioner, our refrigerator and many others. We had two new cars, but one or the other was continually in the garage or not running.

Those kinds of attacks can weaken a marriage relationship, meaning it won't take much to start an argument. That's where we were. Very little money, everything breaking, and God was revealing that He wanted us to have life more abundantly.

I remember during this time that a terrible rainstorm came. We were living in a house on a mountainside in San Diego, California. The rain was rushing down the mountain and working its way under our driveway. If it didn't stop, we knew we would lose the driveway, which would mean we had no way to get from our home to the street. These attacks had weakened us, and we were in the middle of an argument as the storm raged around us.

Suddenly, we saw the trick of the enemy! We could clearly see what he was doing to us. We could see the end result (a lost driveway). Immediately we asked for forgiveness. We got into agreement and started praying that our driveway would be spared. The storm ended, and we didn't lose the driveway.

The Father's concept of time is different from our concept of time. Jesus taught that all we have to do is ask, and we will receive. *"Until now you have not asked for anything in my name. Ask and you will receive, and your joy will be complete"* John 16:24, NIV.

So we know God's Word is true. We know we have only to ask, and we will receive. We know the enemy desires to sift us like wheat and that when we vow to live better and to enjoy the blessings God has for us, the devil tries to trick us into failing. We *know* these things! And still, when the attacks come, we sometimes falter and stumble, and we begin to doubt all that we have learned.

God knows this is human nature. He warned us many places in the Scriptures that the enemy would deceive us. God is patient. He waits for us. He stands behind us, walks beside us, and speaks to us in the night season, reminding us that His Word is true. He does not move on our behalf just because we have a need. He moves in the direction of our faith and obedience. He has taught us to believe, to expect, to know that His love for us is great and His promises will not fail.

I have a perfect "right now" example of the enemy's efforts to get us out of focus, to keep us from accomplishing God's will in our lives. I was in the process of writing this book when I noticed that the automatic cleaner we keep in the toilet tanks wasn't working properly. We just recently moved into this home and put those blue cleaners in all the toilet tanks. As I reached to take it out, I realized it was simply plugged. Suddenly that bright blue cleaner went all over my walls, my carpet and my hands. Even as I write this, I am looking at blue hands and fingernails.

All this was a trick to distract me. I am writing it to say the enemy doesn't care how he gets us discouraged or causes us to lose focus, just so he accomplishes his purpose. We have to remember the Greater One lives in us, and the devil has no power except that which we give him. Needless to say, I cleaned up my mess and continued to write this book with my blue-green hands. I won, and the enemy lost.

My hope is that you will now be prepared for the enemy's attacks as you move toward God's perfect will and begin to dedicate your marriage, your home and children to His kingdom. Knowing the attacks will come is a distinct advantage. We can prepare. We can put on God's armor. *"Finally, be strong in the Lord and in his mighty power. Put on the full armor of God so that you can take your stand against the devil's schemes. For our struggle is not against flesh and blood, but against the rulers, against the authorities, against the powers of this dark world and against the spiritual forces of evil in the heavenly realms. Therefore put on the full armor of God, so that when the day of evil comes, you may be able to stand your ground, and after you have done everything, to stand. Stand firm then, with the belt of truth buckled around your waist, with the breastplate of righteousness in place, and with your feet fitted with the readiness that comes from the gospel of peace. In addition to all this, take up the shield of faith, with which you can extinguish all the flaming arrows of the evil one. Take the helmet of salvation and the sword of the Spirit, which is the word of God"* Ephesians 6:10-17, NIV.

From the moment the devil deceived Eve in the Garden of Eden, God had his number, and He has kept us informed. Essentially, there is nothing to fear. We can read the Word, learn what God desires for us or from us, and become new creations. Then, knowing the enemy is coming, we can put on the whole armor of God. That is the ideal way. If you panic when the attacks come, you will lose your focus and forget your vows and your good intentions.

The Lure of the Past

When things get challenging, Satan is quick to remind couples of the way things used to be when their marriage was in disarray. He loves deception. Remember what he said to Eve in the Garden? *"Now the serpent was more crafty than any of the wild animals the LORD God had made. He said to the woman, "Did God really say, 'You must not eat from any tree in the garden?'"* Genesis 3:1, NIV. He knew that wasn't the truth, but it fit his purposes. And that is the way he comes against us when we try to give our homes and marriages over to the Lord.

Sometimes the people around us may not want our marriages healed. Maybe they are unhappy in their own homes. Maybe they fear they will lose our fellowship, so they encourage us to go out socially, or join in behavior that isn't good for any marriage. Such people will be quick to jump into the situation, reminding the husband or the wife of things that were said in the past, of things that were done. They will criticize the new decision, the new dedication, saying it won't work, it can't work, or it's too late.

If you and your spouse stay in agreement about the changes you are making, you will be able to withstand this kind of attack. Put on God's armor and you will be able to quench every fiery dart from the evil one. Refuse to listen to any negative word about each other or your marriage. Some people expect marriages to fail or, at best, to be miserable. All day, every day, we are exposed to the world's concept of marriage. The morning DJ's offer jokes, insinuations, and outright jabs at marriage as we drive to work.

Those attitudes frustrate me when I hear them. I know they trigger doubts, suspicions and memories in couples that might already be struggling. Once you leave for the office, once you are away from your spouse, from the new commitment, from the Scriptures, prayer time and promises you have made, you may be vulnerable to attack. The devil will assault you with negative thoughts. *"What is he doing right now? Cheating again? Laughing at me? Are the children safe? Did she just go back with me for the money?"*

It takes *all* the armor of God to resist these attacks. Memories have power. They play pictures through our minds, and they remind us of the way we felt when our marriages were failing. A person can leave home excited and pumped up about the newly restored marriage, and just a few hours later return home battered, defeated and doubting every promise and pledge.

If you feel this happening, when you realize you are under attack, call home and ask your spouse to pray. It doesn't matter how many miles separate John and I. When attacks come, we get on the phone to each other; we talk about what is happening, and we bind the tricks of the devil. Agreement, sharing our feelings, standing together against all circumstances and helping each other during these times only makes our marriage stronger.

That's a good practice whenever a spouse has to spend a lot of time away from home, especially if they work in ungodly or secular situations where there is a lot of temptation. They need to gird themselves before they ever walk out the door. The Word says, *"Therefore take up the whole armor of God, that you may be able to withstand in the evil day, and having done all, to stand"* Ephesians 6:13, NKJV. That means, when we think we have done everything in our power to stop the attacks of the enemy, we need to start all over again and withstand him anew.

Even children become uncomfortable when relationships go through transition. If a husband and wife have had a dysfunctional marriage, the children have probably grown accustomed to playing one against the other. Will they like the new order in the family? They may not. They may whine, cry, plead, throw tantrums, and anything else they can do to get their parents to fall back into old behavior patterns. Don't worry. They'll soon realize the benefits of the restored family relationship.

Renewed marriages have strength enough to send the devil scurrying for whatever weapon he can find to break the power. Couples need to realize as they begin the rebuilding of their marriages that the greater the attack, the more powerful their reconciliation is going to be. Every day should begin with agreement, prayer, and putting on their armor. Those three things can seem difficult when a marriage is hurting, when it is struggling just to survive. But, remember God meets us where we are.

There will be countless opportunities to fall into old patterns of selfishness, stubbornness and control. There will be many times when misunderstandings could lead us into old behavior and cause us to react in anger, doubt or mistrust.

Some of those emotions and feelings are habitual, simply things we have felt so often that it is normal for them to resurface. When they do, we need to remind ourselves that we think differently now, that we have new commitments, new promises, and new goals. If they persist, or when they nag at us, causing doubts and suspicions to rise up, we have to realize we are under attack.

Godly marriages, lived as the Lord ordained, have unbelievable benefits. That is why the enemy does not want us to experience them. Would we be vulnerable to his tricks, to his temptations, if we were as happy as God planned for us to be? No. Would we find sin in its many guises: adultery, cheating, stealing, and arguing, attractive if we were reaping the rewards a godly life brings? No.

This revelation should help us. God's plan for our marriages, for all our relationships, will bring freedom, joy, satisfaction, and fulfillment. The devil's plan is just the opposite. It produces dysfunction, unhappiness, unrest, quarreling and depression. It's up to us to choose God's plan. Deuteronomy 30: 19-20 says, *"I call heaven and earth as witnesses today against you, that I have set before you life and death, blessing and cursing; therefore choose life, that both you and your descendants may live; that you may love the LORD your God, that you may obey His voice, and that you may cling to Him, for He is your life and the length of your days..."* Deuteronomy 30:19-20, NKJV.

That should make us realize how completely the devil blinds our eyes at times. We may *have* the Word available to us, we may even understand the Word when we take the time to read it and ponder what it means. But what do we do with that knowledge? Look at the numbers! Look at the fruit. The world is filled with people who walk around, shackled by sin, never knowing the boundless joy God planned for them.

People allow the enemy to steal their marriages, their deep and abiding relationships. And once he gets the marriages, the children of those unions follow. This is bigger than one of those high stake poker games in Las Vegas. This battle is for our hearts, our destinies, and our souls.

The amazing thing is the totality of the devil's attacks. He is able to convince millions of people that they are clever enough, sophisticated enough, and intellectual enough to see through religion. It reminds me of a person standing on a ledge in a burning building. There are firemen below with one of those nets to catch him if he will only jump. But fear says, "What if they drop me? What if I miss?" Even though he will surely die if he stays on the building, he is afraid to take the leap.

The world wants us to think that Christianity is a leap—a frightening jump into something unknown, controlling, and downright dangerous. They want us to think Christianity requires us to give up everything that is fun. Surprisingly, hundreds of thousands of people believe just that. They never realize that they have been manipulated by the enemy, that they have been cheated out of a birthright that was given to Abraham thousands of years ago. *"And I will make your descendants multiply as the stars of heaven; I will give to your descendants all these lands; and in your seed all the nations of the earth shall be blessed..."* Genesis 26:4

If the enemy is willing to come against entire nations in order to get them to disregard that promise, imagine what he is willing to do to stop a husband and wife from turning their entire marriage and family over to the Lord. He will use any form of deception he can find to make them fall back into old habits, to make them doubt the promises of God, and to make them decide that it is just too hard to put their marriage back together.

Don't get me wrong. It is hard. It takes a level of dedication that many people have never reached before. But the rewards are worth it. Have you ever heard army buddies talk, men who have shared a battlefield together and who have literally had to rely on one another to survive? There is a level of trust that develops during battle, a kind of bonding that is rarely equaled. Husbands and wives who manage to withstand the attacks of the enemy, who resist, overcome and find victory for their union, will discover they have developed the same kind of bond as those soldiers.

So attacks will come. Be ready. Remember that every healed marriage produces healed children. Healed families are mighty warriors in the Kingdom of God. In the end, if you remain steadfast in your commitment, many in your family will probably come to the Lord. It is more common than not to see entire families saved eventually after just one spouse, child or teenager finds the truth and begins to live a godly life.

When I got filled with the Holy Ghost and made Jesus the Lord of my life, my oldest child, Yvette, wanted what I had, and she started getting up early every day, reading the Word and praying. The change in my life changed her.

One of the families at my church was brought into the Kingdom in just this way. They had a son who was difficult. He was one of those children that got into trouble at school; he hated authority and even tried shoplifting. He smoked and experimented with all kinds of rebellious activity. His family struggled to find ways to help the child, but they looked in all the wrong places. They never went to church. They had no Christian friends to advise them.

They took the boy to secular counselors and things simply got worse. Finally, in desperation, when the boy was twelve, after he'd gotten in a lot of trouble at school, they moved to a rural area in another state, hoping to get him away from the group of friends he had chosen and give him an opportunity for a fresh start. This only made the child more angry and rebellious, until he met another boy on the school bus, and the boy invited him to church.

It is my opinion that sometimes children caught up in extreme rebellion are simply looking for a way out of it. They are looking for a leader, an example, someone who will say, "Hold on a minute. You stop right now." That is what happened with this young man. He met a pastor. He met a man who told him about another man. That man was Jesus.

The young man was able to give his anger, his rebellion and his willful disobedience to Jesus. It was easier for him than it was for his family. After years of living with the boy's temper and explosive behavior, his family did not believe him. They watched. They waited. As his mother says, "We knew he would fail. We just didn't know when." But he didn't fail. He became a powerful youth leader in that church. He began to preach. He began to produce good fruit. One by one, his parents, his sisters, his brothers-in-law, nieces and nephews all came to the Lord. Today that young man is an associate pastor, and he works with troubled youth.

Imagine how the enemy must have tried to stop that chain of events from coming to pass. He didn't just lose one angry, rebellious boy to God; he lost the boy's entire family! He lost every individual that family will ever talk to and teach about the redemptive love of Jesus.

So resist the enemy's attacks. He wants to cheat you and your children out of the inheritance God promised to Abraham. He wants to see you lose your marriage to deceit, arguments and selfishness. The last thing he wants is for your entire family to find Salvation, to rise up and become all that God knew you could be even before you were born.

Chapter 11

Bringing Your Marriage Back Into Order

Once a couple realizes their marriage needs the protection and blessing of God to achieve all it was intended to achieve, they can begin to address the things they need to do to bring about change. The degree of work they will have to do is in direct proportion to the amount of honey that has leaked out of their honeymoon.

How long has their marriage been under attack? Have hurtful words caused wounds that are slow to heal? Are the children caught up in the drama, taking sides and keeping the home in an uproar? Have stubbornness, selfishness, and control issues been given dominance and power in the home?

All of that dysfunction, all of that pain and hurt will have to be given to Jesus. And it has to be a deliberate act. The husband and wife have to get into agreement; they have to visualize actually laying their troubles at the foot of the cross, giving all of their problems to the Lord. That doesn't mean they have to be in complete agreement on everything at that moment, just in agreement on the fact that they want to save their marriage. The other issues will come together in time, as they stand fast, refusing to return to bad habits and refusing to submit to old behaviors that never brought anything but hurt and pain to their home and their marriage.

I've learned that it sometimes takes a long time to fix everything. Without the grace and mercy of God, it would be impossible to heal many of the traumatized marriages we have created. There are so many things that have to be forgiven. Cruel words, infidelity, selfishness, hard-headedness, and all the other things that punch holes in a couple's relationship and cause the honey, the love, the passion and affection they once had for each other to gush out onto the ground. But God is waiting. He can heal every wound and rekindle flames of love.

We can take a lesson from the bees. In nature, when winds or animals or even humans have damaged a beehive, the bees are quick to respond. Swarms of workers rush out to repair the damage, mending tears and making certain the honey won't be lost. Why? The honey is the lifeblood of the hive. It provides the food and the energy that keeps the hive's population alive.

So is the honey in our honeymoon the lifeblood of a marriage. It gives us the strength to overlook flaws, quirks and mistakes. It makes children feel loved and secure; it is the healing salve that God has provided to families in order to make husbands and wives feel appreciated, valued, and adored.

We have looked at a lot of examples in this book of the things that can happen when we let all the honey drip out of our honeymoons. Now I want to talk about the path back to healing. God is so good. He knew how much work it would take for us to keep our marriages on track, so He warned us of the devil's tricks; He gave us witty inventions and ideas for defeating the devil, and then He gave us the gift of Salvation so no matter how seriously we messed up, there was still hope. When Jesus died on the cross, He died for all our sins. He died for the insults and sarcasm we would hurl at each other. He died for the infidelity that some of us would commit. He died for the selfishness, the stubbornness, the lies and the poor stewardship that would force many marriages and relationships to the brink of collapse.

By His stripes we are healed. Not just physically. Sometimes I think people forget that God's perfect healing covers so much more than disease, broken bones, and disfigurement. God's healing is for marriages; it is for relationships between parents and children, between friends, co-workers, and people who go to church together. God is the greatest healer of all time. Once you and your spouse bend your knees before Him, once you give Him permission to enter your lives and set things in order, He will move on your behalf.

To bring healing to a marriage, a couple must spend a lot of hours in prayer. Prayer encourages intimacy. You will be more forgiving and more willing to maneuver through the changes that will be required of you if you submit everything to God. You need to ask Him to reveal areas in your lives where you have to change. You each need to let the other one honestly tell you the habits and behaviors that have eroded the marriage and allowed the honey to drip out.

If you have never developed a pattern of being in agreement on important issues, now is the time. As you learn to agree in prayer, to agree on the things you desire for your marriage, to agree that no matter what it takes, you will see the crisis through to victory, you will find you are rediscovering things you love about each other.

There are so many ways to go about revitalizing a marriage. All of them take work. I would suggest that both spouses commit to complete honesty. When a couple has avoided intimacy and communication for a long time, it is very difficult to reestablish those habits. Now is a good time for a date. Maybe a nice dinner, soft music, some time alone. Perhaps at first, you could limit your conversation. It's enough to know you both want to make your marriage work.

You could dance, touch, try to remember the things that used to make you laugh. Maybe each of you could tell something about the other one that used to make you weak in the knees, that helped you fall in love.

If it's difficult to talk, other things, more intimate details, desires, and expectations, could be handled by writing them down. You could decide on a number of important questions and issues that would help you reconnect and understand each other. Once you've written those questions down, I would suggest you sit together and pray. After that, you could take some time to answer the questions. How have your views of marriage changed? What do you want now? What do you hope to achieve from a happier marriage? What would make each of you happy? What is required if the marriage is to recover? Are you willing to make significant changes for the sake of your spouse, the sake of your children, and the sake of your lives together?

It really helps to know what the expectations are. Now you can read each other's responses. This will generate conversation, guaranteed! You will have to commit, before you read the responses, that there will be no criticism of the things written. No comments like, "Well, if that's what you wanted, you sure picked a bad way to show it."

After you've read the responses, you need to pray again, to ask God to help you become the husband and the wife you want to be. Ask Him to give you patience, love and understanding, to help you reach new levels as Christians and as married people. Believe it or not, that first part, as tough as it sounds, is the easy part. Next you have to start to live it out, to literally put to a test that Scripture that says, "*I know that nothing good lives in me, that is, in my sinful nature. For I have the desire to do what is good, but I cannot carry it out. For what I do is not the good I want to do; no, the evil I do not want to do—this I keep on doing. Now if I do what I do not want to do, it is no longer I who do it, but it is sin living in me that does it*" Romans 7: 18-20, NIV.

Why is change so difficult? Because old habits don't want to die, and behavior patterns are persistent. In many cases, people are used to operating and answering out of offense. They are used to feeling slighted, offended, neglected, and angry. They are used to communicating through sarcasm, insults, negative expectations and hurtful remarks. When you lay all that mess down, you have to get into agreement that you will no longer function that way in your marriage.

So what attacks can you expect? Well, the first and most obvious is that almost every remark and event will push old buttons. If he calls her to tell her he's going to be late, and he once cheated on her, she will most likely have to fight an urge to doubt and accuse him. What if she has a history of nagging and being very bossy, and she tries to make a suggestion about something new? He may have to fight an impulse to ignore her or to tell her she's being a nag.

You will need God's most tender mercies. Old habits cling to us and pop up, even when we have determined we'll have victory over them. Old behaviors *will* have to change. That is absolutely vital. A lot of wives can be bossy, and it is embarrassing to men to have them act that way in public. Understand, I am not saying *men* should be bossy. But I do know there is something about the male ego that can create great embarrassment for men when their wives' constantly tell them what to do.

Male ego can be difficult for young wives to understand. Our husbands like to do things for us, and they certainly want us to think they can do anything. When John and I were very young and eating out one evening, I couldn't open the ketchup bottle, so I innocently asked the waitress to do it for me. That insulted John, and he asked me never to do that again.

Of course, that male pride can go too far. Men can be too controlling. They may embarrass their wives and their families by correcting them in public, by refusing to let them participate in activities, and using fear as the chief method of control in their homes. That is not godly, and it certainly isn't scriptural. How does God say a husband should treat his wife? *"Husbands, likewise, dwell with them with understanding, giving honor to the wife, as to the weaker vessel, and as being heirs together of the grace of life, that your prayers may not be hindered"* 1 Peter 3:7, NKJV.

Good husbands are strong men who have enough confidence in their own character and abilities that they do not have to bully their wives or their children. And good wives are confident women who do not have to control their husbands, embarrass them in front of their friends, or manipulate and connive to get their way. Changing these old negative behaviors will be imperative if a husband and wife want to submit their marriage to God's will.

So let's recap what we've talked about so far. To bring a marriage back into order, you must get into agreement on every major issue, you have to submit to prayer, and you have to make a serious commitment to overcome old habits and destructive behavior. Being human, and habits having the kind of tenacious strength that they do, it is possible that one or both of you could backslide. If that happens, when one of you lashes out in anger or falls back into a behavior you have agreed to stop, there has to be complete forgiveness.

Forgiving each other every day is crucial. We know that once we repent, God forgives us so completely that He never remembers our transgression again. But we are not God. We have a tendency to remember things, even after we have forgiven people for them. I don't think we do it out of spite, but rather because we haven't matured in our Christian walk. As soon as a similar event occurs, when we get offended anew, we have a tendency to suddenly remember the old offense. Women seem to be especially guilty of that. I have heard many men say that nothing equals the power of a woman's memory.

We need to read and remember the 'love' scripture as often as possible. *"Love is patient and kind. Love is not boastful or proud or rude. Love does not demand its own way. Love is not irritable, and it keeps no record of when it has been wronged. It is never glad about injustice but rejoices whenever the truth wins out. Love never gives up, never loses faith, is always hopeful, and endures through every circumstance"* 1 Corinthians 13:4-7, TLB.

But whatever our habits have been before, once we commit our marriages fresh and new to the Lord, we must forgive each other for all offenses, old and current. We cannot afford to let our new promises to each other be sidetracked by the devil's efforts to entangle us in misunderstandings. This is the point when the enemy will pull out all the stops. He does not want any marriage to be recommitted to the Lord. He does not want healed homes, happy children, and contented husbands and wives. If there are alarm bells in hell, I suspect that every time a couple decides to rededicate their marriage to God, it sounds like an air raid down there.

So agreement, prayer, an honest assessment of what each spouse wants and expects from marriage, followed by a determination to give up selfishness, stubbornness and controlling behavior, and an unwillingness to get caught up in misunderstandings and unforgiveness, is the best way to start on the road to healing a marriage. I have talked with couples that devised all kinds of ways to defeat old conduct. They came up with code words that would stop them from slipping into negative past behavior. They invented gestures and warning signs for moments when something happened that used to generate an argument.

There are other things you can do to protect your marriage. You need to let family and friends know that you have made a new commitment, that you intend to be each other's best friend, that there will be no room for criticizing or talking about your spouse in front of you. That is a bad habit that relatives can develop. Maybe a wife has shared too many details concerning the things she and her husband have fussed about. Maybe a husband has complained to his father or brothers about his wife's nagging or her unreasonable demands. These family members get into a habit over the years of freely joking and teasing about these issues. But that is dangerous. It erodes the husband's and wife's bond, and it certainly cannot be good for in-law relationships.

If you are making an effort to heal your marriage, you cannot allow others—family, friends, or coworkers—to interfere in that union. Even if it means telling people point blank that their comments or jokes are no longer welcome. And it is surprising the impact that kind of loyalty will have on others. They will respect the marriage in a way they never have before. They will immediately have a different idea of that home and that relationship.

Before I end this chapter on ways to bring a marriage back into order, I want to talk about couples already involved in second or third marriages. The Word has been used to beat such couples over the head in the past, and there are still churches that incorrectly interpret certain scriptures and use them against people.

God meant for marriages to last a lifetime. He did not intend for people to trade in spouses the same way they do boats, cars, and houses. But there are times when marriages are not saved. There are abusive situations that cannot be tolerated. And there are situations where marriages have operated so far outside God's law and His instruction that the offended person simple cannot recover. If a husband cheats on his wife over and over again, she may reach a point where she can never trust him again. The same with a husband whose wife has been unfaithful. Betrayal hurts, and it is difficult to forgive.

So we find ourselves in a world where many of our couples are in second or third marriages, and where the children in the home might come from both former relationships plus a few from the new union. That is life. And it is life with a battery of built-in problems, prejudices, and self-doubts. Many couples hate to admit to their new church that they are involved in a second marriage. They have good reasons. Maybe they've been hurt in the past. Maybe they've been overlooked for positions of leadership because a church took the 'religious' position that leaders should be men who have had only one wife.

Let me just open that can of worms and go there. *"Now the overseer must be above reproach, the husband of but one wife, temperate, self-controlled, respectable, hospitable, able to teach…"* 1 Timothy 3:2, NIV. *"A deacon must be the husband of but one wife and must manage his children and his household well"* 1 Timothy 3:12, NIV. *"An elder must be blameless, the husband of but one wife, a man whose children believe and are not open to the charge of being wild and disobedient"* Titus 1:6, NIV.

The Apostle Paul lived in a time when there was a different attitude toward women and toward marriage. While some of his speech might seem prejudiced about women, even sexist, he was quite a liberal in his time. He advocated a lot of female leadership in the early churches, and we know there were deaconesses in his organizations. Was he talking about men who had several wives? Was he talking about divorce and remarriage? There have been many different interpretations. But it is fair to say that those scriptures have been used to beat up a lot of good Christians over the years.

What does God expect? He expects husbands and wives to love each other and to dedicate their homes and their children to Christian principles. When marriages fail, when a man or a woman takes a new spouse, God is not in the background ignoring that new spouse, still pushing for the failed union to be revived.

Some couples are already in a second marriage before they get saved and involved with Christian living and commitments. What do we do then? They are brand new creations. We cannot and should not hold anything from their past against them. God doesn't. The Word says, *"Therefore, if anyone is in Christ, he is a new creation; the old has gone, the new has come"* 2 Corinthians 5:17, NIV!

Well, it's clear to me that couples that are already involved in second marriages when they get saved, are quite married to each other in God's eyes. And God is no respecter of persons! We know that. *"Then Peter opened his mouth, and said, Of a truth I perceive that God is no respecter of persons"* Acts 10:34, KJV. The New International Version says it this way, *"Then Peter began to speak: "I now realize how true it is that God does not show favoritism...."*

We cannot think it is right to admit some people completely into the body while we hold others outside (those who were already saved and members of the body of Christ when their marriages failed). That makes no sense at all. In this day and age there are many people, even pastors, who have been through divorce. We know it is not God's 'Plan A' for anyone to have that experience. And we also know that once a couple marries, even if they failed to wait for the special person God intended for them, they should do everything in their power to make that marriage work. But sometimes that is not enough.

Because the world is filled with second marriages, third marriages, blended families, stepfamilies and all kinds of extended families, we are going to see all those kinds of families in the church. And that is a good thing. It means we're still doing what we're supposed to do. We're telling our coworkers, our family members, our friends and our neighbors that there is a better way to live life.

As these families come into the church and begin to use their gifts, talents and callings to serve the Lord, we need to be clear on a few things. God loves them. He has forgiven them for not making a go of their marriages. He has sent the memory of all their former sins and failures into the sea of forgetfulness, exactly as He did for all the people who have had only one husband or wife. Now He wants us to get wisdom on how best to deal with the problems of stepchildren, blended families and custodial and non-custodial parents.

These are the areas where our brothers and sisters in Christ will need help. No matter how much they want to serve the Lord, they may still stumble as they try to understand how best to discipline a stepchild—a child who perhaps is only a member of the household on weekends. Maybe they will need to talk to someone about feelings of insecurity when they are constantly measured against Daddy's new wife or Mama's boyfriend. If marriage isn't for sissies, let me assure you, second marriages are REALLY not for sissies. There are so many issues that couples never even thought about before.

Sometimes a child gets angry every time a new husband and wife embrace. There can be feelings of jealousy in blended families that were practically unheard of in the past, when nearly all families consisted of the original mom and dad and children. We need to create support systems for today's families, a network where couples that have wisdom and expertise in a given area are willing to share that knowledge with others.

The world changes. I'm sure if we were to look at family life as it was commonly lived while Jesus was on the earth, we would have a hard time recognizing it. Then, and for a long time after that, women and children were considered property. Children were not pampered and indulged like they often are today. Actually, most people struggled just to survive. They couldn't afford the luxury of coddling a child.

But today things are different. We have time-saving appliances, computers, and all kinds of machines that make life easier. Most families don't have to raise crops in order to eat when winter arrives. We have more time. We have more money. We don't love our children more than our ancestors did—we're just able to show it more.

Churches and church families need to recognize that times have changed. What was once considered normal might not reflect exactly what we see today. But, whatever we are used to, we need to understand that God loves and respects the families that come into the Kingdom with a few bruises, bumps and holes in their armor. We need to help them. We need to honor them and utilize their gifts and talents in the carrying out of the Great Commission.

So, bringing marriages back into order, salvaging all the honey from their honeymoons, is important for all marriages. We do not ever want to add to the difficulty a couple faces by insinuating (or coming right out and saying) that their marriage is inferior because it isn't a first marriage.

It is not easy to stop, regroup and to rebuild a marriage. Any couple that is willing to undertake that challenge is to be admired. And supported. Once they tell us what they are trying to do, once they have committed to standing by each other, defeating the enemy and building their marriage stronger for the Kingdom, we all need to help them in any way that we can.

Chapter 12

Reaping the Harvest

The Bible has many references to reaping the harvest, and we clearly understand that God sees this as a time of reward, a time when He pours out His abundance, and people can relax and simply enjoy their bounty.

"For the LORD your God will bless you in all your harvest and in all the work of your hands, and your joy will be complete" Deuteronomy 16: 15, NIV. In the Old Testament, references to *harvest* generally referred to crops and to bounty that people could bring into their barns. In the New Testament, almost all references to *harvest* are actually talking about people and our responsibility to bring them into the Kingdom.

But in this chapter I want to focus on harvest as a time of rest from labor, as a reward time for those who have been faithful enough to see their marriage relationships through to their golden years. In the beginning of the book, we talked about marriage as it was meant to be. And then we talked about the things that come against marriage, the issues and the attacks and all the temptations of the world. Even in those early chapters I mentioned that God saves the sweetest honey for last. That is never more true than in our marriages.

A great peace usually attends marriages of long duration. There is familiarity, a confidence that the other person's actions and reactions are already known and loved. For most couples, all the arguments and struggles are in the past. Often people say couples that have been married for a very long time even begin to look alike. They can finish each other's sentences. They know every like and dislike; they anticipate each other's needs and feelings and emotions.

All the best that God designed for marriage can be clearly seen in couples that have reached their senior years, still together, still in love, and reaping all the rich rewards the Father promised. *"They will still bear fruit in old age, they will stay fresh and green, proclaiming, "The LORD is upright; he is my Rock, and there is no wickedness in him"* Psalms 92: 14-15, NIV. *"Even to your old age and gray hairs I am he, I am he who will sustain you. I have made you and I will carry you; I will sustain you and I will rescue you"* Isaiah 46:4, NIV.

God did not intend for us to be frail and incapable of enjoying life once we reached our golden years. He promised we would be *fresh and green,* and that *He would sustain us.* How blessed are those couples who commit their lives and their marriages to the Lord. Not only do they have a loving helpmeet beside them throughout their earthly journey, they have long life and a Father who carries, sustains and rescues them. God grants these couples friendship, comfort, strength and a peace that makes their eyes shine and their countenances glow.

Remember in the early part of the book when I told you about two poems? This one was also written by Perry Tanksley, and it expresses my feelings for those marriages that stand the tests of time.

Golden Years

Our latter years are called
The golden harvest years,
For gold is very precious
Wherever it appears.

And whether owned by kings
Or workmen earning wages,
Gold always seems to grow
In beauty as it ages.

Our springtime years are sweet,
And bright is summertime,
But only golden years
With autumn splendor shine.

If you are one of those couples that are steadfast and have managed to go the distance, you have a lot to offer younger husbands and wives. Perhaps you could teach classes in your church, willingly share the secrets that brought you to such a point of grace. In addition to all the things you have grown to enjoy in common in these later years, you can also say along with Paul, *"I have fought the good fight, I have finished the race, I have kept the faith"* 2 Timothy 4:7, NIV.

Another benefit that couples that have stayed together for many years can enjoy is their shared children and grandchildren. This is no small feat in a world where more than half of all marriages end in divorce. Understand, I'm not trying to take anything away from second marriages and blended families. But there is a deep joy and satisfaction in enjoying grandchildren together. Families that have that privilege are blessed with a sense of continuity, with a heritage that the enemy has managed to steal from others.

During our lifetimes, we see a lot of honey come and go. Remember when we talked about there being a honeymoon period with marriage, new babies, new homes, new jobs, and every other experience that a couple shares? I have not only had all those kinds of honeymoons in my personal life, but in my pastoring life as well. New pastors always have a honeymoon period with a new church. I have experienced that many times with John, but also as a pastor myself.

Couples who stay together, who protect and guard the honey in their honeymoons, become masters at repairing the tears and holes and cracks which life, other people, and outside forces have tried to inflict on their marriages.

These husbands and wives have managed to shield the honey in their marriages, in their families, at work, with their friends, and also in their churches. They have survived all the new babies, the tremendous-twos, teenagers, first dates and having a child maneuver out of the driveway for the first time. Most of them have dealt with children in rebellion, with children in love and with watching their youngsters leave the nest one after the other.

They are survivors. Although they gave much love and affection to their children, once they all left home there was still plenty left to sustain them as a couple. They kept the honey safe; they didn't let it drip, run, or be stolen away.

Most of the long-married couples I know learned early on that a good marriage would take a lot of work. They invested in themselves, in each other and in their families. They stewarded over their marriages in the same way a responsible person stewards his money. Most of them still hold hands. They like to be together. They enjoy their honey, and they refuse to grow too old to enjoy the love that brought them together.

They have learned not to go to sleep while angry with each other. That practice is guaranteed to let a whole lot of honey seep away. But because these couples dealt with their anger and their frustration and their doubts before they fell asleep, they never allowed those things to grow to be big problems. Because most of them submitted their marriages to the Lord, they have been able to reap the benefits of God's perfect plan for marriage.

Marriages that reach their golden anniversaries are marriages that have borne a lot of fruit. There is the fruit of children and grandchildren. There is the comfortable fruit that comes from years of loving, trusting, and knowing each other. There is the fruit of aged honey, the realization that everything done to preserve the marriage was a good investment.

The things we went over in this book, the scriptures we read, and the cautions and warnings we discussed, are things that long-married couples have mastered. They are good teachers. They have a lot of wisdom, and most of them make excellent fruit inspectors.

Young couples would be wise to go to these older husbands and wives for advice. They should observe them, see how they treat each other, how they still grab hold of hands or look deep into each other's eyes. Long-married couples usually laugh a lot. They don't take themselves too seriously. They have learned that doing something thoughtful and pleasing for each other brings as much joy as doing something for themselves.

These couples have absolutely refused to settle for less than God's best. They have read and understood His will for their lives. They have let the principle of agreement guide them day in and day out, year in and year out.

What did it cost them to give so much to each other over the years? I'm sure there were many times when they each went to a restaurant or a movie just to please the other one. Times when they went without something they wanted, in order to purchase the desire of the other's heart. Times they bit back impatient or angry words in order to keep the peace.

And what did they gain?

Peace. Long life with a friend they love dearly, a friend who knows every touch and every part of them, who would literally lay down their life to see them safe and happy and well. That is a wonderful thing. What does the Word say about that kind of relationship? *"Two are better than one, because they have a good return for their work: If one falls down, his friend can help him up. But pity the man who falls and has no one to help him up! Also, if two lie down together, they will keep warm. But how can one keep warm alone? Though one may be overpowered, two can defend themselves. A cord of three strands is not quickly broken"* Ecclesiastes 4: 9-12, NIV.

That three-strand cord is often referred to as a husband, wife and the Lord. There is a great deal of strength in that combination. A husband and wife who are in agreement, who trust God to keep His promises to them and to help them achieve all the goals they have for their marriage and their home will not be easily defeated by anyone. Especially not the devil.

These are the end times. While no one can say exactly when Jesus will return, it is safe to say that many of the signs He told us to watch for are present in the world today. We do not have time to waste. Those of us who are married need to make certain we are living together as God told us to live. There is no time for insisting on our own way, no time for selfish arguments, manipulation, and all those other behaviors that steal honey from our marriages and cause pain and confusion in our children.

We do not have to live that way. We can read the Word. We can make it a point to understand God's plan for our marriages, and then we can live exactly as He says. Wouldn't it be wonderful to end our seasons on earth with all that honey still safely stored in our honeymoons and our homes? To see it safely deposited in our children and those around us, confident it wouldn't leak and flow away?

God knew honey was a wonderful thing. "Then their father Israel said to them, *"If it must be, then do this: Put some of the best products of the land in your bags and take them down to the man as a gift—a little balm and a little honey, some spices and myrrh, some pistachio nuts and almonds"* Genesis 43:11, NIV.

He referred to honey as one of the best products of the land. Honey is thick and rich; it coats, covers and embraces, a perfect substance to surround our relationships. It is sweet. It is good for us. In Exodus 3:17, the Word says, *"And I have promised to bring you up out of your misery in Egypt into the land of the Canaanites, Hittites, Amorites, Perizzites, Hivites and Jebusites—a land flowing with milk and honey."*

How wonderful that God equates leading us into a land flowing with milk and honey with bringing us out of a miserable situation. Honey is good for us. It relieves the suffering of the past and it eases our misery. Knowing that, we should be even more dedicated to protecting the honey in our honeymoons.

"...until I come and take you to a land like your own, a land of grain and new wine, a land of bread and vineyards, a land of olive trees and honey. Choose life and not death" 2 Kings 18:32, NIV! In this scripture, the Lord compares going to a land flowing with honey and other good things to choosing life over death. That is so exciting. Throughout this book we have talked about choices, about how poor choices lead to death and good choices lead to life. Here we have confirmation.

So I say one more time, choose life. Make those choices that will redeem your marriage, uplift your children and set your spouse on a road that leads to a land flowing with milk and honey. Protect the honey that coats and sweetens and covers your honeymoon and your home.

Choose life. Then live it to the fullest. That is what the Father desires for us every day of our lives.

To contact the author, write:
Pat Avanzini
P.O. Box 917001
Ft. Worth, TX 76117-9001